SMALL TOWN/ BIG TOWN

Growing Pains on California's Central Coast

IRA JAY WINN

iUniverse, Inc.
New York   Bloomington

iUniverse books may be ordered through booksellers or by contacting:

iUniverse
1663 Liberty Drive
Bloomington, IN 47403
www.iuniverse.com
1-800-Authors (1-800-288-4677)

Because of the dynamic nature of the Internet, any Web addresses or links contained in this book may have changed since publication and may no longer be valid. The views expressed in this work are solely those of the author and do not necessarily reflect the views of the publisher, and the publisher hereby disclaims any responsibility for them.

ISBN: 978-1-4502-0944-1 (sc)
ISBN: 978-1-4502-0945-8 (ebook)

Printed in the United States of America

iUniverse rev. date: 03/24/2010

Testimonials:

Including photo essay:
   Impressions of the California central coast around San Luis Obispo
      By Ira J. Winn

Sources: Unless otherwise noted, most of the articles printed herein were published in the San Luis County Tribune (formerly The Telegraph Tribune). Previously unpublished articles from the period 1995-2009 and those recently written for inclusion in this book are noted as *unpublished*.

The author gives special thanks to the three fine Tribune Opinion Page editors with whom he has worked over the past fourteen years: Warren Groshong, Bill Morem, and Stephanie Finucane.

CHEERS TO THE MANY CO-VOLUNTEERS WHO
WORKED AND CONTINUE TO WORK TO PRE-
SERVE THE BEST IN URBAN DEVELOPMENT
AND A SUSTAINABLE QUALITY OF LIFE.

THE AUTHOR, SUMMER 2009, HIKING IN THE DAKOTAS"

About the Author

Ira Jay Winn is Professor (Emeritus) of Urban Studies and Education at California State University, Northridge. He is the author of two other books:

THE EDUCATION MIRAGE (iUniverse, 2003) and

BASIC ISSUES IN ENVIRONMENT (MERRILL, 1972). His writings on environmental topics and social themes have appeared in a variety of national and international journals and magazines.

Over the course of Winn's career, he served as educational planner in Brazil, training specialist with Peace Corps, environmental education fellow with the German Fulbright Commission (Bonn) and the Environmental Protection Service (Jerusalem), adult education specialist (southern Africa Fulbright) consultant to the Laramie Energy Technology Center, and National Endowment for the Humanities fellow in American federalism. He was educated at the University of Illinois (Urbana) and the University of California (Los Angeles)

He resides in San Luis Obispo, California where he serves as a volunteer mediator for Creative Mediation and the state Superior Court.

Contents

PREFACE

On the central coast of California, some twelve to fifteen miles inland from the cool waters of the Pacific, is the city of San Luis Obispo. It sits in a still largely agricultural area, a mecca for grapes and wine, vegetable, fruit and other marketable crops, as well as cattle and dairy.

The area is home to the campus of California Polytechnic State University, with its twenty four thousand students and faculty. San Luis Obispo (or SLO as it is known) is the county government seat, a fulcrum of business and commercial life that daily draws from near and far thousands of commuters to work as well as to recreational, and cultural ventures. It is also home to two economic engines: a huge Men's Colony prison and a PG&E nuclear power plant. SLO is roughly half way between San Francisco and Los Angeles and is a main line stop for Amtrak passenger and freight rail.

Our city has an enviable reputation, rated by national magazines as having one of America's most pleasant downtowns. It is marked by creek-side walks, a landscape of rolling high hills and the remnants of higher volcanic peaks, a variety of public art, busy galleries and shops, quaint restaurants, coffee houses and other watering holes, and places to sit and discuss issues of the day. But it is a town in faster transition than ever before, with all it means for better and for worse. More people, more cars, more malls, more tax base and taxes, more infrastructure, more costs. More!

More is not always better, nor is it always worse. But "more" brings with it a range of problems as a city transitions from small to big. It is all too easy to throw away the charm and ambiance of a unique town in a headstrong rush toward "development" – whatever that comes to mean in terms of copying the patterns and bringing on the problems associated with larger cities that churn dollars much faster than San Luis Obispo.

At stake are balanced growth and a healthy environment that protects and nourishes a lifestyle fast disappearing from California. There is a tasteless sameness as smaller towns rush to copy each other and imitate what has become commercially fashionable. Newer trends in city design and planning, based upon hard lessons learned from multiple mistakes, are unlearned, overlooked or forgotten.

There are lessons to be gained from this transitioning process and from the assault by such forces in San Luis that equate bigger with better and almost any growth with progress. These lessons beg to be shared with other towns facing similar dilemmas of development, just as SLO can learn from many cities combating negative trends and influences. Half the problem is a reluctance to learn or to change because of the tendency to do business as usual. The pressures of a money-first economy are easily evident in towns throughout California and the nation.

* * * * * * *

After many years teaching urban studies and education in the Los Angeles area, and a few years after I retired from the university, my family relocated in 1995 to San Luis Obispo, just after an economic upturn began on the Central Coast. We bought the very first house we were shown. And only a month after settling into our new home, I was approached by an old friend, who asked me to substitute for her and write a "Greenview" column on any environmental topic for the local major newspaper, The San Luis County Telegraph Tribune (later shortened to the SLO County Tribune); she was over-committed and unable to take her turn among several columnists who were committed to the project.

And so it began, a steady infusion of my articles, letters and commentaries on environmental and related issues that caught my eye

– mainly local city and county questions of growth and development, but equally focused on social priorities and issues of values –and even some off-beat or humorous forays. Most were published, and most of all in the Tribune, but some appeared in other local publications, which I note when appropriate.

To better organize this book, I have divided the articles among topical themes, rather than chronologically, and I have made some editorial changes. I've up-dated a number of essays and changed some article titles to those I had originally submitted, and have included a number of previously unpublished pieces that I wrote during this period of time (1995-2009) which reflect wider ranging interests in the world. Now, some fourteen years after I began writing Point of View articles and letters to the editors, I have compiled my thoughts into SMALL TOWN/BIG TOWN: GROWING PAINS ON CALIFORNIA'S CENTRAL COAST.

Participating in the local community has been a healthy learning experience, even as I developed somewhat of a reputation for being a gadfly to local government, calling it as I honestly see it and enjoying the dueling with those who have different views or who simply do not comprehend the long range implications of continuing with political business as usual. A cadre of other critics joined in this task, but the views expressed here are strictly my own. I note that I discuss some county-wide issues because many stem from and are part and parcel of the city and environs.

I respect the importance of a mix of viewpoints, especially on complex issues for which there are no easy answers. I keep myself open to listening to contrary arguments while reserving the right to put forth my own critical analysis. Also, I have honed my listening skills over the past years by serving as a volunteer mediator with Creative Mediation and the San Luis Obispo Superior Court. Obviously, not every issue of importance has attracted my written involvement or attention, the drawing down of groundwater resources, especially on the Nipomo Mesa and north county, and the long and nasty Los Osos sewer dispute being two major examples.

In SMALL TOWN/BIG TOWN I hope to underscore what is at stake in preserving environmental balance in the city and surrounding countryside. We all owe this to the next generations, even as we stand on the shoulders of those who preceded us. The battle for freedom and sanity in a growingly complex, technological age cannot be won by political couch potatoes or off-the-wall fanatics. And despite the many flaws discussed here, our town so far remains a sometimes teetering but charming place. Let us agree to respect our differences and to accept the need for honest and critical analysis. And now I invite you to read a wide ranging urban-environmental perspective that aims at challenging your interests, sensibilities, and sense of humor and outrage.

Ira JayWinn, is a resident of San Luis Obispo, and Professor (Emeritus) of Urban Studies & Education, California State University, Northridge. He was educated at the University of Illinois (Urbana) and the University of California (Los Angeles).

I: LOOKING BACK
AND MOVING ON

SEEKING RELOCATION? CALIFORNIA'S CENTRAL COAST IS THE BETTER CHOICE

It was time to move on. After 38 years living in Los Angeles, minus a few years of overseas assignments, I had retired from the university, gone on a lecture tour to China, and had settled into an all too comfortable routine in one of the beach suburbs.

Yet, L.A.'s pulsating traffic and crowding, the constant nervous tension of a city on edge about crime and earthquakes, about pollution and deteriorating public services, compounded by the sheer frustration of trying to get anywhere without harrowing highway hassles had dulled the wonders of the City of the Angels. On the surface all felt normal, but deep within my psyche discontent was stirring. With retirement, a major change was coming due.

Though somewhat insulated from many of the city ills, living as I was but a mile from the ocean, life had become too humdrum. Some lines from a poem by Hermann Hesse, which for years had been tacked up over my writing desk, called to me: "... From deadening habit he can find salvation, who gladly leave and set anew his sail. For us the call of life will never end; be strong my heart, take leave and find new breath."

So in February, 1995, we put our house up for sale and began to evaluate as relocation possibilities all the many towns and areas we had visited both in the U.S. and abroad. Quickly we decided to stay clear of cold weather, keep to California because of its beauty and variety, and at last came to focus on Marin County, just north of San Francisco, where we had some good friends and which we had known as a center for cultural ferment and easy approach to exceptional parks and recreation. Or so we felt at that time.

Many well-meaning friends warned us about the pitfalls of transplantation -- the loss of roots, the comfort of the familiar etc., but the call to make a change was too strong. In the midst of a very difficult home sale, we moved temporarily to a lucky find, a nicely located condo in San Rafael. We began a three-month stay filled with house-hunting and intense exploration of Marin —the community centers and health clubs, the hiking trails, the wineries, the parks and headlands, the access to San Francisco and the East Bay, and the other cultural amenities that inspire and activate retirement.

We sought an active town life, rather than retreat to distant suburbs, gated walls, or pretended squire-hood. And for a while, the excitement of change and adventure gripped us. Besides, with California Proposition 90, approved by voters in Marin and a few other counties, we could transfer our low real estate tax base; having lived in the same house in Los Angeles for twenty-one years, we could save thousands of tax dollars with a move to Marin county. It all felt too good to be true – and so it was!

First disappointment was the housing stock, dilapidated in even supposedly affluent areas, plus outrageous prices very much akin to the situation in Los Angeles. A two or three bedroom fixer house would stick us with a huge mortgage plus years of patching and renewal; my back had grown too old and too wise to go through all that again. Of course, we could have chosen to move further north near the Sonoma County line, but the towns we checked out there were bedroom communities and mall-dominated drive-throughs, largely lacking in visible signs of life. I'd be buried in those places before I died.

A second critical flaw is Bay area congestion. With little or no planning for greenbelts, scattered communities had sprung up on rich farmland and eventually spilled over and joined into one huge megalopolis, with different names. Rampant urban sprawl has desecrated the land and shows little sign of ending. The San Francisco Bay area laughing at L.A. is a classic case of the pot calling the kettle black.

As the suburban goo has leap-frogged north of the Golden Gate bridge, quick access to and from Marin has become unpredictable. The main 101-freeway corridor is often a giant parking lot of creeping cars, idling engines, frustrated motorists, polluted air. The main access streets of once lovely San Rafael and other feeder communities are strangling with traffic, while the downtowns are fading despite some valiant efforts to stem the flow of business to the freeway-centered malls. In many parts of Marin county, streets and roads are broken and deteriorated as a result of neglect and deferred maintenance. Marin still has some of the most wonderful natural and cultural amenities in all of California.

But if getting there is half the fun, Marvelous Marin has little to laugh about and a lot to reconsider.

And reconsider we did, as it dawned on us that a move from L.A. would not be that much of a change. We decided to investigate the Central Coast, where we had friends living in the college town of San Luis Obispo. Memories of beautiful hilly terrain and a dynamic downtown drew us south from Marin, and within a very few days of exploration we bought the first house we were shown.

The rest is history, and we revel in our choice of home and community. From a quality of life perspective, it made far more sense to choose San Luis Obispo, which boasts:

- Easy and quick access to the surrounding natural environment, and a wide variety of interesting recreation.

- A friendly and dynamic downtown filled with good restaurants, bookstores, meeting places, shops and interesting places to explore –all easily walk-able.

- A mix of age groups and an environmentally concerned and cultured citizenry.

- Better climate than Marin, with winters some 7-10 degrees warmer, and ample rainfall –but not the overly wet and cold winters of northern California.

- Several good libraries and a nearly completed major performing arts center. A city that appears in balance, on the move, and so far not opting to join the stampede toward the overbuilt and under-planned.

In short, Marin towns have many of the advantages of San Luis Obispo, but they lack easy access and the distinctive character and flow of our city center. SLO town is nationally recognized for its charming and vibrant core. In the scoring of places to live actively and be inspired, for me it is now San Luis Obispo 9, Marin 4.5. Viva San Luis. We love your heart!

ijwinn

A RILED READER WRITES FROM THE
SAN FRANCISCO AREA

Perhaps your gripes are twenty-five percent correct, not such a bad indictment of any city or geographical area. But that leaves you seventy-five percent wrong! If your patronizing article dissuades others of your ilk from moving to Marin and the Bay area we owe you a debt of gratitude. It's a shame you didn't take more Yuppies back to Southern California when you left. At least Marin has been spared from yet another outsider whining about the cost of housing.

Mr. Winn failed to heed his friend's warnings. If he could not afford a house here, then why did he (try to) move? As a professor of urban studies, he should understand that urban sprawl began in the Bay Area before California was a state. Real estate values are high in Marin because of the large amount of open space. While I don't like overcrowding and freeway congestion, either, I have no sympathy for Mr. Winn....

Marin does have problems, but I am tired of interlopers trying to change Marin into whatever dreadful place they just left. These are the same type of people who want another coffee shop downtown, as if two to six were not enough, and who want to convert cottages into castles, destroying the character of towns.

Like much of the United States, Marin suffers from post-World War II eradication of railways in favor of automobiles. Marinites are finally suffering from the short-sightedness of voting against BART (Bay Area Rapid Transit). At least, the 101 rail corridor may actually be reopened. Problems with improving infrastructure are also not exclusively Marin's, and these problems are at least being discussed. We need residents who will be part of the solution, not hypocrites who whine about problems they help create.

Although some of Mr. Winn's complaints are valid, some of his boasting about San Luis Obispo is inappropriate. From most locations in Marin, the surrounding environment, parks and open space can be reached on foot or by bus. Marin's aware and cultured citizens have preserved a large portion of our natural environment, which is much to blame for the high real estate values. There is also, as Mr. Winn writes, "a dilapidated housing stock in the most desirable areas" because people don't have a better place to move. While Marin may have only a junior college library in the county, there are numerous university libraries accessible by public transit such as UC Berkeley and San Francisco State. If Mr. Winn had done some research, he could have located a dozen city and county libraries. Also, there are many performing arts venues here and in San Francisco that can be reached by public transit. Ferry service is available for those who don't want to get stuck on the Golden Gate bridge during commute hours.

I grew up in Marin and spent most of my life here. Most of the changes I have witnessed have not been positive. As our population achieves maximum density, our quality of life is adversely affected. Marin has failed to keep up with improvements to infrastructure, and planning is typically short-sighted. A countywide disregard for historic preservation also has adversely changed the character of many towns. Despite these problems, Marin is still better than other places I have lived or visited.

As for you, Mr. Winn, one less resident is an improvement for Marin. You will not be missed.

EVEN PAST THE GOLDEN GATE,
IT'S CHAOTIC & BADLY PLANNED

Both my Marin and ex-Marin friends and I got quite a chuckle out of the apoplectic response to my article on why I chose not to retire in the Bay area. Oddly, the writer agrees almost fully with my diagnosis of Bay area and Marin ills (congestion, overcrowding, dilapidated housing, bad planning, transportation chaos) but gets lost in his tantrum over the fact that the argument is made by a member of that dreaded species – a SOUTHERN Californian!

A silly chauvinism makes for fine venting, but also leads to an ignorance of some basic facts and a misreading of my intent. It was not to twit Marin, but to point to some important lessons in planning for other cities, including San Luis Obispo, not yet in Bay Area stagnation.

Marin's crowding does NOT derive mainly from expatriates from Los Angeles but from enormous spillover from San Francisco and the Bay area. Scape-goating plays the crowd, and is absurd. I would guess that there are just as many ex-Marinites living in southern California as there are southern Californians living in Marin.

The complainant's listing of the libraries and cultural advantages of Marin only underscores my own writing that, "Marin still has some of the most wonderful natural and cultural amenities in all of California." L.A. can make the same boast. But the problem for Marin, as for Los Angeles, is the supreme difficulty of getting anywhere, given the freeway chaos and the poverty of good transportation planning—to say nothing of the energy loss and time wasted driving to, say, the Berkeley library from towns such as Fairfax many miles away and across the San Francisco Bay.

My arguments favoring viable and dynamic downtowns of human scale is not so cleverly turned on its ear by ranting about "turning cottages into castles" and "destroying the character of towns." Some towns such as San Luis retain a unique character, while others remain or become insipid. Indeed, a Marin housing planner telephoned to congratulate me on the accuracy of my article. More than a few Marinites and Bay area residents have said the same.

Finally, let me explain that I could afford to pay average and slightly above Marin prices for a house. My call on housing is not sour grapes at all, but a consumer's right (and duty) to reject grossly over-priced, shoddily built, and poorly-maintained properties, whose only claim to a high price derives mainly from area snob appeal and a gross shortage of housing stock.

Building code enforcement in Marin seems about as lax as street maintenance. L.A. has at least tightened and enforced standards. The beautiful architect-designed house I ended up purchasing in San Luis Obispo would put to shame 80 percent of the houses I investigated in Marin. A similar property in Marin to the one I purchased on the central coast would cost almost double. And I can be in a lively town or out in the wine country or beaches in ten minutes from San Luis city.

The easing of Marin and Bay area problems lies in combinations of light rail, much greater provision for duplexes and tri-plexes, village neo-traditional planning, and an outright ban on automobiles in some congested places. This is bitter medicine for some, but it is better than doing little to solve the problems or keeping with the present patterns of "development."

I do have some sympathy with this reader's rebuttal to my article. As he is a partisan for north San Francisco Bay living, and the admittedly unique big metropolis south across the bridge, I can better understand his need and his comfort in defending the San Francisco area. Time will tell a fuller story.

TO PRESERVE THE ENVIRONMENT
YOU MUST HAVE REFEREES

No sports fan would think it fair or sane to play a major ballgame or sport without the active presence of umpires or referees. One can just imagine the bloody chaos that would erupt in the stands or on the field of play if players themselves were to decide what's fair or foul. Yet, many of these same fans, who fully accept the logic of requiring referees for something so elementary as a game, see no illogic or impracticality when it comes to the much larger and more complex "game of governing". They feel that somehow American society can run by itself without the active presence of national referees for environmental and other protections.

Much of the public lacks historical reference to past breakdowns in social order, and seems fogged by illusions, fallacies and general talk-show nonsense. Indeed, "environmental wackos" are a scapegoat for a number of talk show hosts, who sometimes dominate the airwaves with their inflated egos. One was heard to declaim against environmentalists for "preferring trees over people." In fact, environmentalists view trees and people as being interdependent, with trees offering both beauty and shade as well as life-giving oxygen to man and animals.

Environmental protection today and a healthy, balanced ecosystem as a heritage for our children cannot be sustained without a set of rules and national guidelines and an executive arm to referee and enforce them. Under both Republican and Democratic presidents, as with liberals and conservatives, our society has enacted a set of rules and protections for modern times that have stood the test of more than thirty years of challenge in the courts – witness the Environmental Protection Act and such enabling legislation as the Clean Water, Clean Air, Endangered Species and Wilderness Acts.

Such laws provide for referees in the form of federal attorneys and inspectors, scientists, fish and game wardens, park rangers and many others whose job it is to carry out the mandates for the benefit of all of the American public. Despite or because of the success of such efforts, bellicose anti-government factions and special interest lobbies are putting forth foolish and short-sighted arguments that American society is "over-governed" and could benefit from a dismantling of federal programs of environmental protection. They are sometimes joined by strident forces in Congress showing favor largely to business interests, who would like to see most federal regulatory power returned to the states and localities (where it could be further chopped up, diluted, made impotent or ignored) – although many states do have strong environmental rules of their own.

The lessons stemming from minimal federal regulation leading to the Great Depression, the repeat lesson of the Savings and Loan debacle of the 1980's as well as the current banking and financial crisis are conveniently forgotten. Similarly ignored is the fact that federal protection and power have flowed into the vacuums left by state and local inaction. National and local needs have been ignored, in part due to state insolvency and in equal measure to laissez faire economics. A sense of stewardship of the land for future generations is too often missing. Five major failures in perspective dominate the anti-environmental movement in America. In no particular order these are:

1. A misinterpretation of the nature and force of urban society as well as a false analogy to the views of Thomas Jefferson.

2. A coincident failure to understand the biological web of life and man's place as a co-dependent player in the world ecosystem.

3. An unwillingness to accept the implications of rapid population growth and technological change.

4. An obdurate insistence that controls on growth and long range planning in general are "un-American" and lacking in benefit to society.

5. A failure to reckon the economic value and long range benefits of pollution controls and related preventative measures.

Thomas Jefferson, a man of incredible intellect, wrote of and from a distinctly agrarian perspective in looking to the growth of our young nation. In his time, the vast majority of Americans lived on farms; the country lacked roads and modern facilities, even for those times, as well as having no major threats to clean water and air. Forests were everywhere, cities few and mostly small, and free land was freely available. Jefferson hated city life and wrote much in support of a sustainable agricultural utopia.

But such was not to be, with America becoming urbanized to ninety percent today. To strike at environmentalism by quoting Jefferson on government ("that government which governs least, governs best") is simply way out of context. Scientist and humanist that he was, Jefferson was hardly the man not to have eventually realized that the times and the land were fast changing and the country required a new, balanced approach to growth and development. The rich tidelands, for example, are already ninety percent ruined from what they were in colonial America. Laws protecting those assets are the true way to pay homage to the man today, not taking his remarks out of the context of time.

In this short essay there is space to remark only on the first and last of the five failures in perspective noted above. The others will be treated in various essays to come on a variety of subjects.

The fifth fallacy of the anti-environmentalists concerns their failure to give appropriate attention to the true economic value of pollution controls as part of environmental planning, a continuing failure that has resulted in over-dependence on fossil fuels and old technology. Very heavy carbon releases are the critical factor in global warming and have startling implications for better health, cleaner air and water, and a less stressful life. With skyrocketing medical costs having dire implications for our national budget, the economic value of shifting to a greener, sustainable economy and investing in pollution-control industries becomes astronomical. For example, the management of the Irvine Industrial Park is southern California, the most successful in the U.S., state flatly that it is because of careful environmental planning and strict controls that Irvine has become a highly desirable place to live and a prime site for industrial location.

Top progressive companies (IBM and 3M to name but two) have cut their operating costs enormously by careful energy planning, often in cooperation with federal and state regulators and utility agencies. Overall energy planning has released billions of dollars to fuel needed economic and social development instead of having to invest those dollars into expansion of additional giant power plants. Today gas mileage requirements for automobiles are finally under careful and belated review as a result of long avoided confrontation with America's dependence on foreign oil.

All of this adds up to a big plus for sensible controls and long range planning. The delusions of the anti-environmentalists are based on short term thinking (and short term advantage) by special interests unwilling to modernize and pay their fair share of costs imposed upon society. Their antics in the Congress and in the states are very costly to the country and counter-productive to a strong economy.

Dollar advantages are not lost on the Japanese Ministry of Industry and Trade (MITI), for example, which has designated "anti-pollution" as a prime economic sector for major investment. MITI, undoubtedly, is amused at the anti-environmental antics in the U.S., which serve to weaken American competitiveness. China too has begun major investments in solar technology and planning toward reduction in greenhouse gases. We had better start reflecting on these facts before foolishly continuing to follow the Pied Pipers of the anti environmental movement and their call for less regulation and planning.

VIEW NORTH ON PALM STREET PAST THE LIBRARY

WE ARE ALL VISITORS TO THIS PLANET

People often speak of forty or fifty years time as though that span of years is so far into the future as to be inconsequential to their lives ands fortunes. The young hardly ever think they will grow old, or certainly don't act that way, and parents often wonder how they possibly could have lost or frittered away all those years gone by. Where has the time gone? Hardly anyone has a good answer. As the haunting refrain goes, "I've let my golden chances pass me by." And so it is with environmental planning and land use.

At a public meeting of the Board of Supervisors of San Luis Obispo County, focused on proposals for development of the Santa Margarita Ranch property, at least one citizen spoke up about what he saw as needless worry about precedents and the future of that development. "Let's proceed with the ranch owners' housing proposal, and simply trust the next generation to figure out how to deal with long range impacts and questions of urbanization. Parents do have to trust their children," he explained.

It all sounded so simple, so easy, until one considers the rapidity of change today, to say nothing of a burgeoning population. Or until one looks at very recent history. For example, it took less than forty years to turn the beautiful and serene ranchlands and citrus groves of the San Fernando Valley of Los Angeles into today's gigantic urban sprawl with its 1.4 million residents. And in the same forty years after World War II, the prime farm and fruit-land of the Santa Clara Valley was similarly transformed into the concrete spread that is the San Jose we know today.

Indeed, in the 1970 retrospective land-use study at Stanford University, San Jose's "self-destruct policies" were duly noted: The marginal farmers, those who didn't like farming or did poorly at it, were delighted to sell their land to developers at inflated prices; the truly efficient and dedicated farmers, however, were by and large forced to sell out because of rising taxes and inflationary costs that were a direct function of urbanization and speculative growth fostered by a City Hall that began in 1950 to make San Jose "the Los Angeles of the north".

Modern technology, symbolized by both computer and bulldozer, plus enormous corporate financial power transcending local and state boundaries have changed the scope and momentum of development. Local politics has lubricated the wheels of the fast changing landscape. Linked with government subsidy and incentives, "development" has come to be rationalized as the essence of national progress and local pride. The blandishment of local control has become a national fig leaf, as the image and reality of copy-cat growth has taken over town after town.

Today's reality gathers force in distant financial centers; it conjures a speeding express train in a growingly homogenous world, a juggernaut gobbling up land and resources and excreting waste and sprawl. Local managers and citizens are enticed by and hard-pressed to go along for the ride. Thus we entrap ourselves in a web of grand plans which take on a life and controlling interest and direction all their own. Can the negative forces depleting open space and limited natural resources be halted and constructively channeled? Perhaps. But in the final analysis nature has its own way of dealing with arrogance toward the land.

Opposition to bad policies and laws, on environmental grounds, is a legitimate strategy and is hardly "anti-progress." The recent example of 30,000 Newfoundland fishermen being legally forced into work-idleness for up to twenty years, while subsidized by the Canadian government, is a case in point. While the Canadian navy patrols the Grand Banks fisheries to prevent foreign fishing vessels from further depleting the brood stock of fish in this once incredibly fertile ocean area, Canadian fishermen are knitting stocking caps while swapping tales of the sea as it once was. The reason?

For almost a generation since the introduction of modern factory fishing, and despite constant warnings from fisheries biologists and wise old-timers, nobody in political power would take the admittedly unpopular step of placing reasonable limits on fish catches in this amazingly productive area of the Atlantic ocean. Finally the Canadian government, in the face of alarming resource depletion, was forced to act at enormous cost to both the province and the country. A similar kind of drama is now being enacted as a preventative measure in U.S. west coast salmon fisheries, with San Luis Obispo county part of a far-ranging suspension of fisheries activity because of over-fishing.

Who then are the real anti-progress elements in this real life drama? Is it the environmentalists who gave adequate and responsible warning of an impending catastrophe? Or more likely is it the fishing industry, which seems hypnotized by short term profits despite the looming extinction of its very own golden goose?

We are all visitors to this planet. The environmental mess that we leave behind for the next generation to deal with surely indicts our traditional way of dealing with our time on earth. We must come to responsibly accept our duty to leave behind a healthy legacy. We must rethink our image of space-time and neutralize our hubris, thus freeing ourselves to act rationally in behalf of our own health and balance and that of our children's children.

WILL PEOPLE CHANGE THEIR BEHAVIOR
BEFORE IT'S TOO LATE?

San Luis Obispo - An old acquaintance breezed into town a few weeks ago and spotted me walking on Garden Street.

Carlo Bottsomeagle is hardly a conventional person, and his thinking is sometimes off the wall. But he is interesting. Ill give him that. And I knew it was going to be one of those bizarre afternoons just by the way he greeted me: "Hey, professor, I'll bet you haven't noticed how dueling is coming into fashion!"

"Dueling, you say? Why, Botts, you old troublemaker, I thought dueling was a dead issue."

"Very funny, Winn. I see you haven't lost your fizz. Well, let me give you a few tips. Dueling is here to stay."

"Really? I thought it ended about the time of the Civil War. Botts, I can't imagine people fighting to the death anymore over real or imagined insults."

"Not ended, Winn, really submerged and hidden. If you read the newspapers carefully, you'll notice that there are always a lot of unsolved stabbings. You see, professor, you can't really change people's behavior, not for long that is.

"Dueling," he continued, "has been around for centuries and there is no way to stop it because it meets people's ego needs. Besides, it's a lot healthier than drive-by shooting or firing rockets from un-manned drone aircraft. Those guys don't even have the guts to face their enemies squarely. The lot of those drive-by cowards would improve immeasurably if they gave their egos a real boost by practicing challenge-dueling. The survivors would gain enormous self-confidence and learn a real skill."

"So, if I understand your point, there is no way to change long ingrained habits. What about the change from large to small cars, then back to big again? Remember when Detroit was spouting the line that Americans would never go for anything less than a huge gas-guzzling V-8? Then along came the Japanese and they really stuck it to us."

"Winn, let's not be naive. Some cars may be shorter, true, but the manufacturers cleverly redesigned them to FEEL like big cars. And it's the feeling, not the fact, that is critical. We're living in a new age, the age of appearances and feelings. So don't try to figure things out just on the basis of facts and science. Did you notice how Congress and the president rushed to up the speed limit on the nation's highways? And this is despite all the safety data proving that speed kills and increased oil consumption wrecks our balance of payments and expands the deficit. But the public goes for speed. It is just human nature and it can't be changed - not for long that is."

"Come off it, Botts. People do change. There are tens of thousands of people breaking the cigarette habit, still more in weight-watchers and hundreds of other self-help groups. They are all trying to change to a healthier behavior."

"OK, they are trying. I'll give you that. But few make it for long, and for everyone who does there are 4-5 kids getting fat and lighting up. Stop seeing change as an individual thing and look at it from the long view of human social behavior. You educators just can't get it. Indeed, you, Winn, are a case in point. I read that you and your friends are all exercised about saving SLO's downtown. You want to keep it pedestrian friendly and plan parking mainly for the fringe of city central. Are you nuts? Don't you know that this is the age of the automobile? Every man and woman is in love with some car. A car is the secret mistress of every American male. It's the ultimate in safe sex, professor."

"Maybe the back seats should be made bigger, like in the old days?"

"Another funny, eh? Well, let me tell you something that you don't want to hear. Walking is passe'. If I had my way, I'd stamp an indelible letter P on the forehead of every pedestrian downtown. I'd have the merchants widen their aisles, and we could drive through and shop without even getting out of our cars. Pay as you exit, and get rid of the sidewalks to boot. ...Well, maybe that's a bit futuristic. But that is how I feel. Make the most of it!"

"Gee, Botts, I'm surprised you are wearing shoes. What would you say to those towns in both Europe and America that are encouraging walking streets and finding that business thereby increases 20 to 40 percent and more?"

"There you go throwing loose facts around again. You professors really slay me...all worried about city planning and the ozone hole and such stuff. You are all too future-crazy about things you can't really change. You need to live in the present, enjoy what there is, and make a buck. You should keep your eye on the till, not in the clouds."

At this point, I could have answered him with examples of how we end up paying many times over for delayed maintenance, and how each generation owes a debt of conservation and stewardship of the land to the generations following, especially given the growing population- but I let it go. I've learned that sometimes it is best not to respond. Instead, we chatted amiably for a while about travel, university days, and then the weather. The subject of climate led us back to the environment and yet another play of verbal swordsmanship:

"You know, Winn, I like you despite your weird idealism. And I'm going to clue you in so you can better grapple with your opponents. Listen carefully. Today, every smart operator will claim that he or she is an environmentalist. The big boys know that you need to declare it publicly- not that you have to mean it, certainly not the way you do. For this is the media age, and it's the glitter of the message, the image you project that is all-important.

"See, you can divide and subdivide this county and state up the gazoo and cover the land with suburban sprawl, so long as you declare that you are doing it in the name of progress and to save the environment. Here are a few examples:

"I'm an environmentalist, but people are more important than owls.

Or, I'm an environmentalist, but we need to attract more carloads of people to stimulate growth. Or, I'm an environmentalist- but we need to expand population to create ever more demand for goods.

"I know these claims can be argued, but that misses the point. The public is taken in by the sound, not the substance. Anyway, the problems that do exist can be solved by eventual new technology or can better be left to the next generation."

"I see what you are getting at. But that positioning is exactly why the younger generation distrusts us so. They see right through our self-deception. In just 40 years of new technology and rampant industrialism, we have upset nature's balance. We've injured or ruined much of the planetary ecosystem on which all life is based: polluted the oceans and the atmosphere, cut down forests, and covered much of the prime agricultural land with concrete. To top it off, we have left little growing room for our kids to make it in the kind of economy from which we have profited."

Botts grew passionate: "World resources exist to be taken and used. It's always been that way, always will be. And problems always have been around to bother the young. It's their job to take up the mantle when their turn comes. Besides there are other worlds to find and explore, once we solve the problem of how to live without oxygen."

"You seem to be doing that now."

"Touche, Winn. But face it, you can't change behavior though the goal may be a good one. You see it's too painful in the short run, and people can't see very far into the future. They'd rather suffer their ills and enjoy their benefits right now, even if it is going to hurt their own grandchildren. At all costs, avoid giving pain, professor."

"In some ways you may be right, Botts. Yet, I believe that things have changed and that a lot of people are trying and others just waking up. When the drought came, we all learned to conserve water."

"Water is all wet and flows easily."

"Yes, I know it hurts to give up old habits and patterns. Even thinking about change can be very scary to many people. But you do make a point and I'll consider taking your advice. I'll try hard not to write anything that might push people to think."

II: SEEKING EQUILIBRIUM

OUR LOVE-HATE AFFAIR WITH CITIES

Why do we love the city, and yet do so much to ruin its heart?

The roots of this great contradiction lie in our pastoral beginnings, our genetic nurturing in the tropical green savanna. Today we are pulled by the power of a world of concrete and steel, giant motors and electronic pulsations. We have become urbane and urban, but our strange affair with the city is one of love and hate.

While living in Brazil, I met a woman who was looking forward to her first trip to the United States- to New York, the city of her magical dreams. When I next met her, shortly after her return to Brazil, she was clearly disappointed. It turned out that her relatives who had invited her lived not in the big city but way out in suburban Long Island on a beautiful estate. She was horrified that the nights were so quiet. She felt "eerie and terrified," and she admitted that she could "hardly wait to get back to Rio de Janeiro" so she could "once again hear the traffic." While Rio is very beautiful, it is also one of the noisiest cities in the world. Yet, she had grown accustomed to the throb of motor vehicles and the screech of tires.

The sociologist Georg Simmel would have had a good laugh at her story. At the turn of the century, he had written about how modern urbanites are overwhelmed with the constant barrage of nervous stimulation. To maintain stability, we simply turn off and try to ignore the continual assault of signals and noise.

But the incessant stimulation becomes self-justifying and even self-fulfilling. Simmel noted that city people become nervous and lonely if left without their familiar turmoil. To remain perceptible, urbanites are nurtured to be forward and even clamorous. The constant pressure and nervousness is both creative and debilitating.

Thus, city people often dream of fleeing to the country, where life is projected to be simple and true- at least for a while. That is why we seek escape to places like rural Montana, the Sierra fothills, or even San Luis Obispo; we wall-in our city yards and houses in suburbias that signal outwardly a search for peace and quiet, away from the hubbub. Hidden away in our fortress-houses or estates, sometimes surrounded by gates and uniformed guards, we try not to wonder what happened to our dreams of freedom. We try not to think about the urban services we demand, or about how isolation is a major factor tearing apart neighborhoods and communities.

I call it the myth of the "make-believe country squire"... the delusion that in an urbanized society we can bring back pastoral life by fleeing to open space and the wild lands. Conveniently we forget that in the process we not only destroy habitat for wildlife, but bring with us all the trappings of city life, which the children then attach to as personal necessities.

Its most absurd extreme is found in campgrounds, where, parked cheek by jowl, loaded with everything from TVs to computer games, the motor-homes growlingly prowl the gravel roads in search of "nature."

But it is in the cities that the country squire is most admired and most dangerous. Dangerous to the city itself. For those 5-, 10-, and 20-plus-acre enclaves are a way of thumbing one's nose at the municipality, while exacting from the city the high costs of roads and street lights, sewer and water, police and fire protection and schools ... to name a few of the services demanded and imposed by peripheral and suburban development; eventually these stretch the urban boundaries, which yields commuter chaos going to and from the now distant downtown.

It is very difficult to convince people that zoning parcels of land for "ranchettes," or subdivision expansion bordering a city, is a prescription for bringing about the very urban mess from which the city escapee is fleeing. In a single generation, population growth both from the landed families and from in-migration will force a continual reduction in lot and parcel minimums. And if you don't believe it, a trip to San Jose or the San Fernando Valley should suffice to prove the point.

Our planet first sustained a billion people around 1820, 2 billion by 1924. Today, a billion people are added every eleven years! Anyone who thinks he can wall his or her family away from that reality is indulging in gross self-deception.

Further, the children growing up in those "anti-urban enclaves" learn automobile dependency as they are continually carted around for city and school services; they grow to adults wanting an equal spread to that to which they have grown accustomed- even as the available land and open space is ever scarcer.

We have to stop fooling ourselves. We need to come to terms with our urban birthright and our stewardship of the land. A growing population will need the best land and more land for growing food. An urban people need a completely different strategy for living a quality life than that ordained in the once limitless land frontiers of the seventeenth and eighteenth centuries.

Progress is not what we cash in on a land deal; progress is truly measured by the environmental legacy we leave to our children! What can we do to prevent insane urban scatter? How can we make our city more livable, more protected and inspiring?

Face it, we need to tighten our urban reserve lines and purchase large greenbelts and reserves on the edges of our city, as wise city fathers from Holland and Austria to Oregon have done in the name of future generations.

This means we have to realize that "highest and best use" of land, particularly prime agricultural land, simply cannot be determined by market price mechanisms that pit urban developers and speculators against rural interests and farmers. By expanding the urban boundary and infringing on open and agricultural land, we inflate the price of land to the detriment of future generations. Good soil, once compacted by bulldozers and concrete, is lost forever! In the process, efficient farmers are forced by urbanized costs to sell out and abandon their craft, while inefficient farmers are only too happy to grab a bonanza and flee to early retirement. The next generation pays.

How can our country, now 85+ percent urban, go on acting as though it is three-fourths rural? Prime agricultural lands especially need to be guarded as a national treasure; the owner-occupants must act as trustees for all future generations of Americans, who will one day either depend upon this food reserve or curse the generation that willfully plundered and sold it.

In its truest sense, priority protection of open land lies at the foundation of a CONSERV-ative property ethic. Urban people with city-bred ideas now control the destiny of the nation. We must re-educate ourselves to modern urban-rural values, and not be drawn in by the dreams of escapists seeking a nineteenth century life as a model for the twenty-first.

Cities are here to stay. A vibrant urban life and a compact and balanced city in tune with nature offers a saner and healthier road to the future than the anti-city sprawl so evident today.

For now, failing prompt and effective action by the Board of Supervisors to draw a line of protection around our rich agricultural-open lands, a ballot initiative will be a required first step to secure regional health. Such a move is already law in several California counties, and is in the talking stage here in San Luis Obispo.

SLO MUST FIND PROPER BALANCE

A number of studies have questioned whether cities can survive the onslaught of the computer and digital commerce. These alarming reports point to a potential fading away of congested (and high-cost) city centers. Why alarming? Because much city planning and business proceeds on the assumption that big downtown office buildings and the infrastructure to bring managers and workers downtown to park and conduct commerce is one of the inviolate rules of civilization. Yet, the financial cost of commuting from suburbs to central city, and back again is staggering. Not only city budgets and taxpayers suffer, but the loss of time and energy and the wear and tear on families is incalculable.

Should San Luis Obispo and other cities be planning for a technology-driven shift that we can but dimly envision? If studies on the horizon are correct, we have to begin thinking in new directions instead of expanding freeways, automobile malls, parking garages downtown, and other stand-byes of the 1950's. At the same time, we must protect the city core as the nerve center of urban civilization.

In 1995 the U.S. Office of Technology Assessment concluded that the rush to computerization is creating "footloose companies" that do not need roots in congested city centers. Urban office towers may become a relic as companies shift to decentralized work stations connected to workers' homes.

As cyberspace grows and decentralization accelerates, downtown real estate values drop; newer work patterns reduce demand for retail, warehousing and office space. Analysts at Arthur Anderson and Co. concluded that a decline of 20 percent in commercial real estate values is possible, thus discouraging new city investment and cutting into the existing tax base.

As electronic connections become more important, personal interactions fade. Manufacturers and software developers are already drawing on highly skilled but low-wage labor in Asia and other places, rather than hire highly paid American specialists working out of central offices in high-cost cities. When work can be done electronically, what does it really matter from where the signals emanate? Besides, televised conferencing exists worldwide, and, when necessary, specialists can be flown in for occasional major meetings.

After World War II, new highways and freeways drained the central cities as people were lured to the suburbs. These corridors were and are heavily subsidized, with cities paying for extension and expansion of public services such as schools, roads, sewers, police and fire protection. Remember, the federal government also contributed heavily toward such services by offering low-cost home loans and mortgage guarantees. The inner cities paid the biggest price in the form of lost jobs, lost tax base, and downtowns empty after dark.

Only a few cities, including ours, survive with active downtowns day and night. Just as the freeways drained the city centers and created a prospering, if extravagantly expensive, suburban sprawl, cyberspace may shockingly transform all metropolitan space. Shopping, banking, schooling, even health care are likely targets of the electronic Net, which growingly affects both suburban shopping malls and services as well as central city

This is a sample of what some experts see on the near horizon. Other observers are much less sure, while skeptics argue that in time the electronic revolution will settle down: Humans are herd animals, not loners. They will demand greater socialization in their work. Yet, is it not absurd to expect people to work set hours in an office given the freedom computerization offers? Can endless preoccupation with electronic screens, whether work or pleasure, be equated with "freedom"?

While no one can be certain of the full impact of changes now fomenting, vibrant towns such as SLO can take great advantage as compared to the big cities. So far, we've been spared the worst of urban sprawl, partly because we have only one interstate freeway. We can still choose to transform our economy, while protecting our environmental assets. But we have to act smart!

What we must avoid is unrestricted growth, a guarantee of urban cancer. Cancer is when the body cells run wild in unregulated growth. What our city does need is balanced, slow growth and much better planning.

We don't need our beautiful downtown to be choked with cars and smog. We don't need our city stretched at the edges with duplicative big malls that simply don't provide high-income jobs or expand the economic pie. Yet, a string of malls is approved here in San Luis, while still others have approvals pending. Where and when does it all end?

Meanwhile, nearby towns have also announced approvals to keep their residents shopping at home rather than in SLO. It is an endless and senseless competition with big-money promises and no winners as the pie is cut into ever smaller pieces. It means long-range recurring costs for infrastructure and the draining of commercial vitality downtown. It leaves us up to our armpits in development that looks more and more like Santa Maria and Bakersfield.

What we do need instead is to take greater advantage of our unique environment and small spaces, linking existing pedestrian malls with attractive walkways and mini-parks connecting offices and stores.

These fit well with an information economy. And we need to put full effort into our new Office of Economic Development to attract entrepreneurs who are leaders in the information-age revolution: environmentally clean, high-paying industry. Quite a contrast to the type of rapid-fire development being encouraged by our present City Council!!!

A year ago, I found a list of 50 Southern California companies that moved to Phoenix between 1991-1995. Why there rather than SLO? Phoenix is notoriously long on stifling summer heat, smog, and year-round impacted traffic and sprawl. Surely, SLO could have attracted at least 3-5 of those companies that would see the advantages of our Central Coast lifestyle.

All over the world exist companies that seek what we have. Let's not block out those possibilities. We can develop our economic base and maintain environmental quality. We can save a quality downtown.

It takes a wiser approach to planning than now rules the roost. Proper balance and intelligent growth in harmony with nature is what the environmental movement is all about. Don't believe in or accept anything less.

CHINESE MINI-PARK AND GARDEN

PERFORMING ARTS CENTER, CAMPUS OF CALIFORNIA
POLYTECHNIC UNIVERSITY

PRADO ROAD IMPACTS JUST PART OF THE PICTURE

Whatever the eventual outcome of the battle over rezoning the Prado land from office to retail, there are important lessons to be learned. For one, the city government cannot treat citizen input as a perfunctory nod to democracy. With all the talk about "community building," community voices must be more carefully considered.

Just as important is the realization that the Prado Road development proposal cannot be viewed in isolation from other development schemes already moving forward or lined up awaiting City Council approval. There are a number of projects that threaten to change forever the character and livability of San Luis Obispo.

The Prado Road plan for big box store development near the 101 freeway is one piece in a total urban puzzle. It is not a simple "land-use decision" that can be compartmentalized and studied apart from the entire urban development matrix. What happens in one part of town inevitably affects what happens in other parts, and this means not only traffic flow, but shopping, esthetics, air quality, and the very quality of life in our city.

As one who studies urban problems, I am particularly saddened by the existing process. The city has sidestepped producing a comprehensive environmental impact report, and the traffic circulation plan offered is not effectual. A pedestrian plan is not even considered a priority. Simply claiming that all major environmental effects can be mitigated is plainly inadequate for any large project, whether a large shopping center or a downtown parking structure. The nature and likely effectiveness of proposed mitigation efforts must be carefully spelled out.

This is not the first time that staff have tried to end-run around the California Environmental Quality Act (CEQA). The City Council needs to more carefully follow the environmental policies in the General Plan for the city, and have the guts to stick to it!

The downtown Business Improvement Association is justifiably worried. The Prado Road proposal threatens its customer base. City approval of the plan would again leapfrog commercial development out of the central business zone. It will create a vacuum downtown as people are drawn by freeway and road to the urban fringe with its giant parking lots and stores. The Council already has scattered malls far and wide, from south Broad and south Higuera to Foothill and Los Osos Valley Road, and has eyes for north of the airport; Broad Street could eventually become an ugly strip mall. Projected developments are 3-13 times the size of existing malls in San Luis Obispo.

Individually each new project claims control of traffic and economic impacts. In any case, it is the *cumulative* effects that are so alarming. San Luis Obispo is in the process of being torn asunder by myriad developments that are fragmenting the city, making it more and more dependent on the automobile, inevitably increasing city tax burdens, and blowing a hole in the life and livelihood of our beautiful downtown. If the goal is reproducing Santa Maria or Bakersfield, we are on the right road. But it is a dead end.

From Paso Robles to Santa Maria the same game is being played. Each city strives to attract more malls and development in the false hopes they will keep home their customer tax base. The jobs produced are largely low wage, and the economic pie is not fast growing. Each competing mall only slices the pie thinner. Only the fast growth of population in towns north and south of here has allowed those malls to survive. Is a huge population push part of the hidden agenda here in San Luis?

The reason the Prado Road mall was initially rejected by our Planning Commission is because that area is zoned for office, not retail space. There are literally dozens of retail spaces standing empty in our city. New, outside investors might better ponder the virtues of locating in such spaces.

Also, we can better spend our tax dollars on health and education and attracting high tech, high-wage businesses, than in pouring dollars out for infrastructure costs for malls and connecting roads. If big money is the game to be played, why not go big-time with Wal-Mart, SLO Bingo, or horse racing?

But seriously, we must remember that tourists and other visitors are drawn here because of our unique beauty and our dynamic downtown; they won't fly here from everywhere to buy products which are locally available for them. And even if they would, it isn't worth sacrificing the character of our town to become a carbon copy of monotonous places indistinguishable from each other. Most of us would not choose to live in San Jose or Santa Maria or Fresno over San Luis Obispo.

I plead against a planning and political process that allows the Council to change set land-use policies established to protect the city and the environment. Because big money development interests have so much influence on the political process, to the detriment of sound urban planning, five cities in California very recently voted to rigidify their growth controls for 20 years so that elected officials cannot fool with the city's long-range destiny. Santa Rosa is one such town besieged with development. Here in San Luis Obispo the warning flags are flying, and Prado Road points to serious flaws in the political process and in the master plan itself.

We as a city and county need to face up to three needs: 1) We must better define and strengthen our master plan; 2) From a regional standpoint, we need strict guidelines that allow for slow and balanced growth that protects the environment and blocks the existing game of leapfrog development and the senseless competition for malls; their redundancy and costs yield city insolvency and urban sprawl; 3) Finally, we must strive to enhance San Luis' uniqueness: a protected downtown economy planned around the full opening of the creekside and a continuation of the pedestrian character of the central core..

Then there is the matter of the proposed freeway interchange on Prado that can't possibly be built in less than six to 10 years. Meanwhile, traffic will stack up on streets adjacent to the proposed mall. It's a circus that will cost perhaps 50-100 million dollars, (in 2009 prices) from Cal-trans, which has not made that project a priority. Other related costs will be borne by the city or, supposedly, by developers.

As one listens to the developers and SLO city staff trumpet the concrete "air bridge" that will span the freeway and someday connect Los Osos Valley and Central Coast malls with Prado Road, eyes roll upward in disbelief. That inter-change will, in theory, be part of a new state highway that will extend Prado Road across Higuera and then flow on to the airport.

It is truly a steel-and-concrete idol, one that opens up the entire south of the city to ever more development and still other roads yet to be born. It feels just like the San Fernando Valley and San Jose, and a myriad of other towns submerged under the bulldozer in the name of "Progress".

I have a much better idea. Build the air bridge not across the 101 freeway, but directly from City Hall to the 101 and then a special lane on to Atascadero State Hospital. There they know how to soothe people who have delusions of grandeur. Another approach is to expel such fantasies and then we can all work together to build a balanced city.

ROCKY COAST AND TIDE-POOLS AT MONTANA DE ORO

HOLD IT! *WHERE HAVE ALL THE RESTROOMS GONE?*

Perhaps I'm terribly old-fashioned, but it seems to me that an acid test of a civilized society is whether or not the citizen can find an available public restroom when in need. In case you haven't noticed, ready access to restrooms between big car-dominated cities , and even within urban areas, is going the way of first class mail.

Why is this? As urban regions becomes more populated, more motorized, and choked with traffic, stalls and unpredictable delays become an ever-increasing part of life. Schedules and plans are thrown awry and nerves become frazzled even as human relations become superficial and often much less civil.

San Luis Obispo County is so far relatively free of such pain, but the future may not be so benign if the mania for rapid development is allowed to prevail. In the big, sprawling cities, one can taste our potential future should city managers allow our cities to spread far and wide and the automobile to dominate our vital heartland. It is then that the fabric of civil society breaks down over seemingly small things, sometimes humorous, usually annoying, and always disruptive.

Once upon a time, companies in large urban areas and in feeder freeways between, vied with each other in attracting customers by boasting of their clean and easily accessible restrooms. Today, too few make the effort, and along freeway corridors between cities one can hardly find a toilet, clean or not. Some places seem to have a permanent "Out of Order" sign on their door. Service stations commonly have a pass-key system that causes agonizing moments of delay at times of great urgency. The nerve of those guys! You have to pump your gas, wash your windows, check your oil and tires… Then, if you're lucky, you might find a place to do your thing. And they have the nerve to call *that* a "service station."

One day I sat down and wrote to several oil companies and a politician. I noted that public facilities do not seem to be the priority they once were, and that restriction of access to restrooms is not a civilized way to proceed. While agreeing that some people terribly abuse restroom privileges, closing the door is not the answer. Better supervision is. Perhaps service stations should be required by law to maintain minimum standards of access and sanitation. Some wise owners take it as a duty to provide the public with facilities both clean and accessible. Government too should make this a required part of highway planning.

Replies to my letter trickled in, all properly sympathetic and, more or less, passing the buck. The plea of the oil companies is that most of their retailers are independent business people over whom they have little control. "However, be assured that every effort is made to educate our people to the importance of maintaining clean and well-equipped restrooms." Of course, education is all to the good. But to the citizen on a hurry call, the only meaningful test is in implementation of the policy.

My political representative had a different view, especially because of my suggestion that the state of California should fund more public facilities. He saw the problem as one of big government vs. private enterprise. The state, he wrote, should not mandate what private businesses should do to assume responsibility for providing facilities on other than state property. His solution was for the citizen to be "selective" in choosing service stations and "to plan ahead" when taking trips. I laughed until my bladder almost emptied.

I wrote in reply: "Sir, your recognition of the problem warms my heart. But nature is not so kind as to give perfect warning. Sometimes you have to go when you have to go! Many states wisely require businesses with significant public traffic to maintain sanitary facilities open to all of the public. Indeed, in Europe such public facilities are simply accepted as a fact of life. This is not really a matter of freedom of choice, rights of property owners, or intrusive government interference. It is purely and simply a matter of civilized living and a recognition of natural biological imperative.

"But since you are unwilling to recognize much more than 'planned toilet stops,' there is, perhaps, an alternative that might fit well with your political agenda. Could you dig up some state money to provide forested watering holes along all state highways, both urban and rural? Willows and birches have insatiable thirsts, and both rhododendrons and azaleas can provide acid-loving screens for the pressured public. Indeed, your leadership on this issue might well earn you the Green vote."

-*New Times, November 28, 1996*

DEVELOPMENT PRESSURES CONFRONTING SLO

A string of development proposals for SLO city and country are lined up like Pacific storms just waiting to explode on shore. Some of these projected shopping developments are as much as ten times the size of our largest existing supermarket malls. They include the proposed Wal-Mart complex in neighboring Arroyo Grande, the Dalidio center adjacent to Central Coast Mall, the T.K. Development (just begun) and the Froom Ranch proposal for Los Osos Valley Road near the 101 freeway. Individually, each new large development claims control over traffic and economic/environmental impacts, a questionable assertion. In any case, it is the cumulative effects that are so alarming.

Our city is being fragmented, made more and more dependent on the automobile contrary to the circulation element of the General Plan, and is gradually being sucked into a process of subsidizing recurrent costs little perceived by the average citizen. These include in whole or part tax burdens inherent to large developments such as overpasses, sewer and water, traffic lights, road maintenance, increased fire and police protection, and the services of schools. Such costs can well overbalance sales tax revenue gains over the long run- figures that cities find embarrassing to admit. And this does not include the negative impacts that will occur as downtown business is dried up by the magnetic pull of huge box stores and giant parking lots on the urban fringe. In good part, the State has aggravated the problem by withdrawing traditional financial support for cities, forcing both cities and towns to look to "creative financing" such as sales tax revenues.

It is a dead-end game. From Paso Robles to Santa Maria the same development scenario is being enacted. Each town is trying to attract more malls and "development" in the false hope they will be able to keep home their own customer tax base, while stealing from its neighbors. Even the jobs produced are largely low-wage, and the economic pie, contrary to wild hopes, is not fast-growing. Each competing mall only slices the pie thinner. Only the fast growth of population in towns north and south of SLO has allowed these malls to prosper or survive.

In other words, what we unwittingly buy with a push for fast-track and copy-cat development is a reproduction of monotonous towns indistinguishable from each other; we play a high risk game of losing our beautiful and precious downtown that is so attractive to citizen and tourist alike. People will not fly to San Luis Obispo from all over the world to buy envelopes or televisions at box stores, however much a bargain, but they will come here to bolster our economy because we do have something almost unique among our towns- a city center that is alive and wonderful, a place to get away from the humdrum monotony of so many of America's cities.

Obviously, we do need to guard our economic vitality in the region and the state. This can best be done by very careful redesign and redevelopment of our economic base, attracting more high tech, high wage businesses, protecting our downtown, insisting on imaginative architecture, and revitalizing depressed and depressing commercial centers. Here it may be necessary to tear down and begin anew.

Equally important to energizing the downtown is the need to fully open up the creekside, including a handsome bridge across the creek under Higuera; then to expand both the commercial and walking areas of the thus expanded downtown. This move, which will take time and careful planning and architectural balance, will keep San Luis a magnet for visitors from all over California and the traveling world. It holds real promise of attracting new business and more tourist dollars than all the vapid development schemes.We must protect our farmlands and our environment from speculative and leapfrog development, and, of course, we must control the senseless competition for malls with their tendency to lead us to fiscal insolvency and urban sprawl.

San Luis is unique as a city and center for county activity, and we must strive to protect that uniqueness. To do this we must reinforce at every opportunity the pedestrian character of the central core. It is the walkability of the downtown that yield a charm and grace, and that radiates a spirit of ease and movement so conducive to psychological well-being as well as commercial vitality. It is the balance between the psychological and the economic that must be sustained and protected.

With our commitment to community health and balance, we can do much to meet these goals with both collective and individual effort. If we want our city to radiate health and harmony, we need to add our voices and our thoughts to the call for renewal.

It is vital to break the frenetic pace and nervous over-stimulation of the big city rush pushed particularly by development interests from outside that are unconcerned with local sprawl and psychological balance. It is our spiritual survival that is at stake as well as our civic duty. *Sierra Club Santa Lucian, July 1997*

ALONG THE CREEK, HEART OF DOWNTOWN

OUR FLAWED DOWNTOWN REPORT

At a cost to the city of $100,000, the Meyer-Mohaddes downtown parking and circulation study is so filled with errors as to be (almost) laughable. In an attempt to appease both the Business Improvement Association (B.I.A.) and the environmental community, it has pleased neither. While the two factions argued at the first city council hearing over costs, revenue-sharing, and what is known as "Traffic Demand Management", the basic planning errors in the jargon-filled technical report slipped by largely unnoticed and uncommented upon. Five huge flaws in the Meyer-Mohaddes (consultant) study undercut its conclusions favoring the construction of 3-8 or more very expensive parking garages in the heart of San Luis Obispo.

The expensive downtown study sets the stage for moving from one costly boondoggle to a $25-50 million string of white-elephant projects to be borne by the citizenry. Let's take a hard look:

1. Failure to correctly identify the retail core area of downtown SLO: The M-M study inaccurately limits the retail core to the area between Osos and Broad streets and from Monterey to Pacific. Very important business and pedestrian areas above Santa Rosa and Johnson streets and south to Nipomo and Beach are strangely left out. The list of stores so omitted south of Broad is striking. Why is this bothersome?

Because, as the consultant freely acknowledges, parking garages should be sited outside the retail core area. Wise city planners have learned that garages, as much as possible, should suck up traffic BEFORE automobiles move into the central shopping-pedestrian zone; cars should not be allowed to dominate and ruin the central core of the city. If the M-M report had correctly identified the full and true retail core from at least Santa Rosa to Beach streets, most of its choices for locating parking garages would be invalidated. Even with the shrunken and arbitrary retail core they project, they make exception for Marsh Street garage #2, which they were ordered to do by the city council. Such is not sensible city planning, but is dictated by politics and a warped vision of our downtown.

2. Division of downtown San Luis Obispo into four artificial quadrants: The Meyer-Mohaddes study divides the downtown into quarters, with a line running down Higuera and across Chorro. This is highly deceptive as the entire downtown core from Santa Rosa to Beach is merely a half-mile. From Palm to Pismo is a quarter-mile. Anywhere in the center is an 8-10 minute walk at most. And what happens in one part of downtown impacts every other part. Downtown SLO is a tiny organic whole, compared to many cities, and it is fakery to assume otherwise. It simply cannot be conveniently compartmentalized. It would be like a doctor telling a woman that her body is divided into four parts, and that she is pregnant only from her knees to her navel!

Why then is the downtown arbitrarily so divided by the consultant? It is to create a convenient excuse for building the Marsh St. garage. Obviously in a city center so divided, it is easy to claim that the northeast portion suffers an acute lack of garage space because of high demand to visit the Downtown Center. The reason that the public loves the Downtown Center is because there are lots of things to do and plenty of places to sit and visit without the intrusion of motor vehicles. The answer to downtown is not to build a string of parking garages at a cost to the taxpayer of multi-millions of dollars, but to build at least 2-3 more downtown centers in <u>different</u> parts of the downtown so as to spread the parking more equitably and <u>not</u> to still further overload an already impacted area. At present, merchants in the south part of the retail core are being cheated by having the focus on parking in the already congested part of down-town. Also, the consultant and the B.I.A. want to be sure to load up the first garage quickly so that its revenue will generate funds for another garage. But let us not fool ourselves: the public will pay with bonded indebtedness (the garages do not pay for themselves in the foreseeable future), and the downtown will inevitably be suffocated by the volume of traffic generated. As there already exist parking garages on the roughly northeast and west sides of downtown, any new garages should be planned for the far edges of the north and south sides.

3. Failure to take cognizance of the effect of traffic generation: There is much discussion in the M-M study of retail sales, garage costs, and automobiles, almost as if the purpose of a downtown is

solely taken up with buying and selling. These are, of course, very important activities, but hardly the only reason for the existence of downtowns. A city center is the cultural hub of the city, a place where people come to exchange goods and ideas, to meet and mingle, to visit museums, theaters, libraries and galleries, and to pass the time in many kinds of productive and leisure activities as well as governmental functions. What draws throngs to SLO's downtown is its vibrancy, as compared to so many sterile cities dominated by malls and, yes, parking garages. The current plan calls for some 2000-plus parking spaces. Each space handles about five visitors a day. More garages means up to 8,000 additional car trips daily into the central pedestrian zone of SLO. If you think traffic on our small surface streets is bad now, just wait. Cars don't target parking from the sky; drivers prowl around looking. And with the downtown choked and smogged, just who will want to come to our city center to buy things or to visit? The Business Improvement Association had better start thinking about that.

4. Failure to ask key questions and misinterpretation of data: The M-M study purports to find a growing parking crisis, but careful review of its own data makes this a highly questionable conclusion. At peak hours, only between 70-80% of downtown parking spaces are taken; in the Downtown Center area, occasionally as much as 90%. But that leaves a thousand spaces empty daily in the downtown. And the Palm Street garage is admittedly under-utilized, especially on the top deck. That deck needs a cover and a skywalk across Palm, descending by escalator to the street below. The Marsh street garage alone should have double fees for entrance during rush times. These relatively inexpensive strategies would free up additional space. But this assumes a severe parking crisis as viewed by the public. Not so. Table 18 of the consultants early report reveals that in random polls taken in the downtown, 73% said there is sufficient off-street parking available on weekends "always" or "most days"; only 13% responded "seldom" or "never." On weekdays the figures drop to 61% and rise to 29% respectively. When large majorities of the public claim no parking crunch, as they did in the survey, it is very upsetting to find the M-M report claiming the opposite.

The M-M report also claims that interviews show that people won't walk more than six blocks, and want to park near their destination.

The SLO core downtown is seven blocks by five blocks, a fact not highlighted. Further, much depends on just how the question is asked. "Do you want to be able to park near your destination?" practically guarantees an affirmative response. But how about: "Would you be willing to walk 3-4 blocks in order to keep our downtown free of traffic congestion and smog?" That question (and other key probes) is never asked by the consultants.

5. Dependence on failed strategy of the 1950s: With its heavy reliance on building costly parking garages, and with only a nod to Transportation Demand Management (T.D.M.), the Meyer-Mohaddes approach is but an updated version of failed traffic planning strategy. T.D.M. requires full commitment to behavioral change through such things as vanpools, shuttle links, staggered workweek, telecommuting, traffic impact fees, and varied parking charges, etc. The unbalanced approach, as advocated by M-M, is inherently contradictory and self-defeating, like trying to run backward and forward in the same instant. Uncertain and sketchy funding for T.D.M., while promoting $20-50 million for parking garages over the next 15 years (much more at 2010 prices), is akin to giving a long-habituated smoker strategies for changing behavior, but then offering him free home delivery of packs of free cigarettes. People simply will not change behavior so long as their old habits of driving and parking are encouraged. Thus, the T.D.M. program, as set forth in the M-M report, is a prescription for failure.

Forward-looking cities, large and small and of quite different geography, are moving toward pedestrian-friendly downtowns and marketplaces, especially as central city garages have not proven advantageous to city life and commerce. The argument that primary dependence on cars will always be the wave of the future is not borne out by history. After all, the same was said about sailing ships and the horse.

Finally there is the serious element of financial risk. The M-M report underscores risks linked to T.D.M. (Transportation Demand Management) but says hardly a word about the much greater risk of huge debts to be borne by the city and taxpayer that are caused by the massive building program proposed. The parking garages do not pay for themselves. They draw on monies from meters and lots, and they require a substantial bonded indebtedness with heavy interest payments for years to come. If one reads the M-M report carefully, one finds an interesting escape-hatch sentence on page 6 of the June issue: "It is conceivable that demand for downtown access and parking could decline with a weak economy and with outside retail competition." Our national and local economy go through up and down cycles, and outside retail competition is a growing fact of life in SLO; it is even stimulated by city councils fixated on encouraging huge malls and acres of parking. What happens when the economy goes into low gear or the new malls draw down business in city center as they are bound to do? What happens when people don't want to come to a downtown choked with traffic and polluted air? The garages begin to empty, but the public is stuck with payments on the bonds. Of course, by then the city council that pushed us to this slippery slope will be long gone; only the names of its members will remain on the white-elephant garages, perhaps on a bronze plaque. The downtown, the heart of our city, belongs to all of us, not just to the merchants who do have their own special interest. But we, the public, must stand up and say our piece now if we are to save the distinctive character and environment of our unique downtown. Unfortunately the city council has gone ahead and purchased Post Office land for the projected garage, even before there is a pedestrian plan in place for San Luis Obispo.

In a travel agents office, I once noted this sign: "Half-price if you know where you are going." The Meyer-Mohaddes Report makes some interesting and valid points, but it simply does not know or ask what *kind* of city we want, just where are we going. It is time to stop wasting our resources and revenues, to build no more than one, perhaps two, parking garages, and these at the far edges of downtown San Luis Obispo. Put much more effort into building 2-3 more Downtown Centers, pedestrian-oriented, festival-type marketplaces, in different parts of the downtown. Connect them with greenbelts and pedestrian walks, and let our city live. Common sense can still prevail. -*Santa Lucian (Sierra Club)*

MARSH STREET SMOKESCREENS

Some leading proponents of new downtown parking garages have orally and in print laid out a number of challenges to me and an informal group of Marsh street garage critics, who sometimes call ourselves, "Saving Our Downtown."

Proponents of more garaging in the downtown core decry the delays in getting the building process started and see our efforts as a waste of time for all concerned. Indeed, they place most blame on a few urban planning professors, who apparently have nothing else to do with their time.

The true reason that the Marsh Street and other garage proposals move forward so slowly has little to do with our advice and appearances before the city council and planning commission. Our recommendations have been largely ignored. The process of environmental review is an essential requirement of state, federal and local law to insure that the city and other governmental entities are proceeding fairly and responsibly, and in the process taking citizen input, which is less a burden and more a civic responsibility.

"Saving Our Downtown" members have correctly warned that the proposed garages would end up costing way over budget, but those obsessed with the Marsh Street site would not listen. We urged lessening the height of the building and finding a different location, where a garage would not contribute to clogging the heart of downtown with automobile traffic en route. Our opponents have turned a blind eye to viable and economical alternatives, which we are willing to support.

The city's Downtown Parking Committee was stacked with garage advocates and business owners who stood to profit from a close-in Marsh Street garage expansion. Long before we "critics" arrived on the scene, the EIR requirement for the existing Marsh Street garage was side-stepped by use of a negative declaration. The environmental reports on the proposed expansion and on downtown access and parking are both flawed. So the stage was set for great controversy and ensuing delays that are hardly the fault of "meddling professors".

The four-story tall box of 330 spaces will dominate its downtown area. Eighty existing parking spaces will be lost due to construction. The city's Cultural Heritage Commission voted unanimously against the Marsh Street addition because of the threat of downtown crowding and being out of scale with the immediate neighborhood. The Planning Commission also voted against it. The garage exceeds city height limits and the weight of the four story building forces very costly concrete foundations for support. Perhaps one hundred and ten, two or three story spaces is all that Marsh Street can afford at best.

Contrary to the argument that people won't walk to shop more than a few blocks away from their cars, countless shoppers eagerly explore the length of the Thursday evening street market in downtown SLO; and they routinely walk even further to football games, concerts, art walks, and other events. Downtown merchants can combine to provide low cost package delivery service for purchased items, thus neutralizing the argument that sales will be lost on heavier items. And certainly thousands of visitors to the summer Mid-State Fair don't hesitate to shop and buy a wide range of things while walking around the huge fairgrounds in Paso Robles.

Our technical volunteers include professors of urban planning and transportation policy, urban sociology and architecture, as well as concerned citizens. More than 1000 people signed our petition for downtown planning review. Perhaps we are a small group- but we are not stupid or unconcerned about the future of our city. We have plans to make the downtown better, and at much less cost to the city. Our ideas have been misrepresented by garage partisans to confuse the public. Here is a brief summary of some of our suggestions:

- Clearing the existing garages downtown of all-day parkers and shifting them to shuttle parking lots. This step immediately frees up 140-plus spaces, each of which will accommodate four to six short time shoppers or more. That's fast relief for any parking crunch, economically smart, and with little cost to taxpayers. It doesn't take years of chasing one's tail to get relief from any parking crunch.

- Constructing a large garage in the Santa Rosa Street area, including a bus depot, a project we have advocated for four years, and which will draw traffic away from the city core. It should be fast-tracked by a city-county special planning team.

- Another distraction and smokescreen concerns the Parking Enterprise Fund. The 32 million dollars it roughly has banked is way under the amount needed to pay for even one garage. The public has to pay the difference, including a bonded debt for loans that will hit taxpayers for over 20 years. Who pays the piper should call the tune. Appropriate placement of parking garages is one huge aspect of construction.

- Finally, we urban specialists see no validity in comparing the formerly moribund downtown to the dynamic conditions of today. In the past it was easy to place a garage or project almost anywhere downtown without great negative effects. Today we have a growing population and modern city problems, especially downtown. We must be very careful to avoid choking the heart of the city.

- The city council can inadvertently drain the core downtown of business vitality by putting malls on the periphery, as we have also warned. Unfortunately the box store/mall genie is out of the bottle, having foolishly not been timely opposed by the Downtown Association. Their reliance for downtown survival on a boutique-centered and upscale "froo-froo" downtown is a dubious venture. Downtown needs careful and vibrant planning, some more basic economic enterprises, an added festival marketplace or two, and a sound transportation strategy. And you can't get that combination with special interest politics ruling the roost.

- Professors are trained to be guided by the facts, not by a booster mentality. After exhaustive study, we have concluded that the facts don't point in the direction of the obsessions of garage proponents. We have no vested interest in this conclusion, and we invite anyone concerned with downtown to listen to and discuss our rationale.

DOWNTOWN GARAGE A SPOOKY NIGHTMARE

To the editor:

I had a dream, a scary Halloween-night panic. Floating over the post office lot behind Marsh Street, I looked down and saw three shadowy figures stirring a huge mixing bowl. It was 10 minutes before midnight and no one else was around.

The moon broke through the clouds and I recognized Council-members Romero and Williams working the paddles.

"Hello, what are you doing down there?" I asked.

They looked up. "Oh, it's you, is it? Well, we're practicing mixing cement to get ready for the new Marsh Street garage."

The third figure moved into the moonlight. It was Mayor Settle. "You too?" I asked.

"Oh, I'm just stirring the pot," he shrugged. "Care to come down and help us?"

I began slowly dissolving into thin air. Just as the clock struck 12, I was able to reply: "No, thanks, my friends. When it comes to that darn garage, I'd rather stay in the abstract than in the concrete."

I wonder what it all means.　　　　Ira Winn

III: HOW MUCH IS ENOUGH?

MORE IS NOT NECESSARILY BETTER

How much is enough? In biology, carrying capacity refers to the wildlife population that an area can support in equilibrium with the environment. Spatial limits and balance also have human implications, which are usually accepted if obvious. For example, the carrying capacity of a soup spoon is what can be brought to the mouth without dribbling; for hand luggage, the limit is weight and volume of the suitcase and what the airline decides is safe.

When it comes to less bounded spaces, however, people seem to forget the idea of limits altogether. We like to think that anything goes. Attempts to apply the concept of optimum use and its corollary, carrying capacity, are viewed as infringements of property rights and "freedom."

We learn the hard way that more is not necessarily merrier or better. Extend the analogy to a much larger space- shopping malls, for example. Here we have special interests at work. To the merchants in the area, more can never be enough. In their perspective, space jammed with people means constantly ringing cash registers. To the City Council, those bells signal a steady stream of sales tax dollars into city coffers. They try to increase this hubbub by placement of huge parking garages in an already busy area. Ten such are planned for downtown in the next decade. So far, it seems, so good.

Sooner or later the downtown area becomes excessively crowded. Surrounding streets are choked with traffic flowing to and from the new garages. Downtown Centre store checkout and theatre lines become impossibly long. Rents rise dramatically.

Eating out in the city center becomes a combat for reservations, a jostling for tables. And a stroll through adjacent streets becomes a struggle. Gone is the delightful ambience of once charming and prosperous San Luis. It's become Anyplace, USA, for the bloom is off the rose.

People become disgusted with the crowded conditions, the endless waiting and hassling. They drift off to the new malls that have, with city and county encouragement, sprung up on the far edges of the city. Without incentive for people to stay in downtown SLO, cash flow slows.

It's an old story to anyone familiar with the life and death of small towns and cities.

Visit Westwood, adjacent to UCLA, to get a good idea of the economic decline of a once-charming and busy village, because of excessive growth, and despite the valiant efforts of a volunteer organization appropriately named "Not Yet New York." Westwood is loaded with parking but quite boring and ungracefully dead.

We begin with the cry of "no limits" and we end up victims of our own delusions. Yet, we can avoid this trap if we are willing to learn from the sad experience of other towns. We must defend our downtown not just for the sake of business, but for its cultural, educational, and government pulse; it is the nerve center for leisurely interchange. Downtown belongs to all of us, not just the business elite.

The future direction of growth in San Luis is southwest. It is the only realistic course for the downtown to expand- toward the intersection of Marsh and Higuera streets. Here is a far more sensible location for a parking garage because it is also close to the freeway ramps, and thus avoids clogging the heart of downtown. It's simply counter-productive to direct traffic flow at parking targets in the midst of an already crowded city center, as stands the current plan.

The Downtown Centre is already at optimum carrying capacity and functions smoothly. We should not throw more concrete straws on the camel's back. A better strategy is to create two or three new cultural and business parks with parking in different sectors of the downtown, enlivening areas long neglected but growing -- thereby spreading the flow of visitors so carrying capacity can be sustained.

So far we retain the magnetism of our downtown. If we think that SLO can "win" a commercial war of attrition against nearby cities and towns by flooding the central city with cars and the outskirts with malls, we are kidding ourselves. We'll just become more like them. Bad development, like bad money, drives out the good. The sales tax dollar war is a formula for monotonous and copy-cat development. It is dictated by big money, and more by greed and back-room politics than by common sense and sound planning. The State of California must learn that bad state tax and fiscal policy is forcing small town growth in awkward and harmful directions.

Perhaps my timing is wrong! The fast-growth scenario may continue in force for years. Then, when we are all hard-pressed by jostling crowds and smelly, snarled traffic, waiting in long lines in some sterile mall in an equally sterile city, will we still smile wanly and even grow to love it? Or have you had enough already?

LOST OPPORTUNITY: DOWNTOWN SHUTTLES

Lost opportunities are like handfuls of gold-dust thrown to the wind. Everyone can wistfully remember roads not taken, golden chances passed by. It's always easier to find ten excuses for not trying something new and challenging than to put energy and mind into a different approach.

San Luis Obispo is losing just such a golden opportunity, a chance to head off traffic problems, save its pedestrian-friendly downtown, and avoid throwing additional millions of dollars onto a garage program filled with contradictions.

Favorable circumstances now exist for changing parking patterns by implementing a shuttle service into the downtown. It would function from two park-and-ride lots, relatively inexpensive to build, which need to be located about a half-mile north and south of downtown. Shuttle bus or trolley service between the ride lots and city center in between them would be rapid and frequent, especially at commuting times.

The park-and-rides would suck up traffic before it congests the downtown. They would provide ample storage, especially for the roughly 175 full-day commuters presently occupying and thus blocking high-demand parking within the existing Marsh and Palm Street garages. This would free those same spaces for approximately 800 short-term shoppers and visitors in need of quick access to the garages.

While other towns move ahead and push for alternative transit modes, SLO seems hung up on warehousing cars within central downtown. Yet, parking management is a third leg of downtown planning. How can space be better utilized and how can parking demand be reduced without further snarling our downtown in garage-bound traffic?

The driving public needs to be taught small changes in driving patterns, aiming at ride lots instead of expecting direct connection to very expensive parking structures that eat up precious downtown space. Driving habits have proven changeable when and where motorists learn the true costs of parking and come to see the advantages of an uncongested downtown – and where alternative transportation is frequent, clean, and safe. The use of park-and-rides is highly successful in a number of cities, including Denver, where, despite windy and wintry weather, people are drawn to the 16th Street shopping and restaurant area, which is closed to all vehicular traffic except shuttles. In city planning, as in business and life itself, timing is everything.

Once a new garage comes on line, devious claims will sprout against park-and-rides. The argument will then be made that ride-lots take away business from the new structures, which will likely not fill rapidly and consistently. Also, city and business employees have "turf interests" in the existing subsidy of all-day, low cost garage parking. Opening up hoarded long-term space in existing city garages must become priority policy now if, as argued, demand is high and supply of space low.

Park and ride, really an old idea, should have been a planning priority five years ago and more.By all accounts, Marsh II will generate 3500 additional car trips daily. This will radiate increased traffic flow into adjacent areas, just as rising garage and meter fees induce more neighborhood parking. Every garage space taken by an employee-parker blocks 5-8 short-time shoppers. The need for shopping is the original justification for new garages. Perhaps the hidden purpose is to subsidize further business and city employee and employer parking? (If so, the garage program is peddled under false pretenses).

Old Town (peripheral residential area close to central city) and downtown ambiance remain at serious risk unless automobile traffic is pulled into ride-lots before it muscles its way into residential and walking streets. Yet, out of 50,000 residents of SLO and despite much publicity, only a handful of people showed up at the Forum to discuss and vote on the exhibits of the downtown access and parking plan EIR. The public remains confused and turned off by the whole parking plan, which has been cleverly steered for four years at least. It's long overdue to lay all the cards on the table and to study the causes of any parking shortages – real or imagined. Without immediate attention to parking demand reduction and management, the fixation on garage-building amounts to a hollow victory for special interests, not for our city or for sound city planning.

Park-and-rides will test the theory that lack of garage space downtown is the cause of retail slowdown, rather than other factors. Once present long-term garage occupants are shifted to ride lots, we will soon learn whether those vacated spaces are actually filled with long-frustrated shoppers. And the park-and-rides will teach us a new and healthy transportation pattern for saving downtown. Isn't that much better than having to suffer crocodile tears over a "terrible parking crisis" that need not be?

(A continuing analysis of the parking puzzle follows:)

DISSECTING AN ENVIRONMENTAL IMPACT REPORT

The Environmental Impact Report of the Parking and Downtown SLO Access Plan is flawed and illogical. The document is poorly organized, avoids key issues, and is misleading. Although couched in lofty goals, the program it endorses can only flood the heart of our city and adjacent neighborhoods with ever more traffic, destroying the pedestrian-friendliness and ambiance of downtown.

Some 3,400 daily additional trips to and from the expanded Marsh Street garage will snake through downtown streets. Up to three more huge garages proposed in this EIR will add another 4,000-12,000 vehicles moving daily in and around the downtown core than is now the case.

The EIR fails to address cumulative effects of traffic generation, virtually assuming that cars will drop innocuously into new garage spaces without negative impacts on downtown streets and people. It's a politician's dream, a citizen's nightmare!

Automobiles cannot fly, nor can they maneuver easily through the core to enter or leave garages wrongly sited in the very heart of our small downtown. Garage placement, as proposed, violates the General Plan and land use guidelines that require new garages be located at the edges of the commercial core "so people will walk rather than drive between points within."

This EIR presents a perfunctory analysis of downtown conditions, making no effort to study the unique draw of central San Luis as a government and cultural, as well as retail center. Like the two paid reports preceding it (Meyer Mohaddes and Rincon), it simply follows the prescribed choices of the City Council and focuses on a pre-selected group of garage sites. The city in effect pays its contractors public funds so they can tell the council what it has already decided and wants to hear.

Little effort is made to look for other alternatives and transit options, to prioritize garage sites, to seriously consider buying or trading for better sites at the true edges of the core; nor is there serious focus on traffic demand reduction and management. It fails to consider the possibilities of limiting garage parking to 3-4 hours, thus freeing up large amounts of parking space for visitors and shoppers who are now blocked by full-day commuter and worker parkers (who could easily be accommodated in shuttle lots).

In May 1998, the so-called "public participation process" drew only 35 citizens of San Luis Obispo and 23 feedback forms. Every alterative plan on display called for one or more garages. Some choice! To draw conclusions about public opinion from this kind of stage-managed show is ludicrous. The truth is the public remains uneducated and confused by the downtown plan, which is a maze of blind alleys and jumbled writing.

A true downtown plan should have come three years ago, and not after expensive studies aimed at modeling the City Council picks.

It should have been an open process with heavy public participation in workshops about the downtown and how to save it from becoming just another sterile, copycat city center. The existing Downtown Concept Plan is dated, reflects views never fully accepted as city policy, and is actually an artistic image of one group that is plagued by the same old parking garage illusions.

The current EIR offers a so-called "No Build" option, which nonetheless includes building the new Marsh Street garage! Three consultants have been ordered to consider that garage as a "given." Suspiciously, it's been fast-tracked and ordered out of the downtown study despite being the worst potential generator of traffic congestion. Some objectivity!

Alternate downtown parking strategies are simpler and much less expensive, but not seriously considered. The EIR fudges the question of supply: For whom are the new downtown garage spaces being built? On one day, we are told it is to draw new customers to invigorate the downtown retail shops, now enjoying their highest success in many years. But on another day, garage proponents swear that parking garages do not increase traffic flow. Still again, we hear that the garages will be built so that surface parking lots can be closed and commercial buildings constructed on those valuable spaces. Supposedly the new garages will absorb the now surface lot parkers. If that is true, it means no new customers, for those people who surface park on lots and residential streets are already downtown.

Then we hear that the real reason is to get people off Old Town and other residential streets, where they are parking to avoid garage and meter fees. Again, no new customers will come from that, and a lot of angry parkers will be attracted into other neighborhoods. Even the City Council voted against a neighborhood parking permit for Old Town for this very reason.

Lastly, where will the visitors park for all the new commercial buildings on former surface lots? The new garages proposed in the EIR will be filled with people who are already parking downtown. Each time I ask these questions of the powers that be, I am met with stony silence.

Far from solving the parking and traffic problems downtown, the plan proposed sets the stage for endless "breeder garages," each aggravating the parking problem and giving birth to still more $6-12 million car parks.

Hopefully you have come to believe that the heart of the city is made primarily for people, and not car warehouses. Let's reject this absurd plan, which threatens the pulse of our city.

Note: Faced with the prospect of having nine to eleven parking garages built in the downtown core, opponents quickly focused on the first such construction on Marsh Street, in an effort to block the "dominoes" from lining up. Nonetheless, the new Marsh Street garage was approved and built as was a second garage, a bit further out from the core on Palm Street. Over the past six years, as the costs of land, building, and infrastructure escalated and the economy deteriorated in response to national and state conditions, the obsession with building parking garages has faded -- but is not dead.

THE OLD MISSION DATING FROM 1772

BUCHON, A STREET OF VICTORIAN HOUSES

AN "OFF THE WALL" CRITICISM

The letter attacking me and my article on urban planning is off the wall, -- but deserves a reply, if only to educate readers about faulty argumentation. The writer is correct in only one respect: I did not write one word about housing in my Tribune piece of Jan. 28, 2002.

My focus was on the process of planning, not on special topics such as affordable housing, Naciemento water plan, education, or many other important issues for which I had neither time or space. Nevertheless, the writer jumps to the conclusion that since I did not write about affordable housing, I must be against it. Is he a mind-reader? In any case, he is wrong. I do have some fresh ideas about housing in SLO, and perhaps one day I will put them to print.

I am criticized for being a "professional immigrant from Los Angeles." Oh my! I pay my taxes here in San Luis, vote here, speak before city council, and serve on committees and as a mediator with the courts and with juveniles. I garden in my backyard. I've taught urban studies for 25 years. Have I lost my right to speak out? Is coming from Los Angeles a new form of original sin? We who live in SLO come from many places. Some of us bring a perspective on urban rot and how to block it, and we are going to do our best to prevent San Luis from going the way of so many towns and downtowns lost to sprawl and greed.

No, I never said, "the whole reason a city grows or doesn't grow should be based on profit, regardless of how it costs the city and its residents." The letter-writer completely misinterpreted my article. In quoting social science studies of growth, I noted hidden costs to the city and an unfortunate and unnecessary tax burden placed on generations of citizens by mistaken schemes and special interest projects that hurt the city and its residents.

You claim "people don't shop in (downtown) San Luis Obispo because it has lousy parking." For some people who hate to walk three blocks that is true, though they'll walk farther than that for a football game or at farmer's market. I might also add that San Luis has poor public transit. Despite all the complaining about parking, in the last five years the downtown has shown amazing growth in retail sales, better than any five years in history. The argument over garaging is mainly one over protecting the core, the heart of our city, much less about new spaces. There is a lesson here if you want to digest it. But you have to be a good reader in order to be a good writer and thinker.

The contention that cities grow by their bootstraps is also not quite true. City and federal subsidies have proven to boost and often warp city growth in ways that cause long range, very costly problems. Good planning avoids that trap, and San Luis can use an infusion of new thinking to invigorate itself. I've put forward positive proposals in a number of areas in print and on the public forum. As my students used to say, you have to put your money where your mouth is.

SHORT-SIGHTED PLANNING WILL TARNISH COUNTY'S CROWN JEWEL

Imagine a building site stacked with all the construction materials to make a house. The residence-to-be lies lifeless, unlivable. Only when the parts are correctly assembled can one assess fully its construction and its value as a house. The assembled building is always greater than the sum of its parts, even as any development must be viewed authentically in terms of its cumulative values.

Planners and politicos routinely review each project proposal with little regard for the whole development picture in the county. Its merits and deficiencies, real and imagined, are carefully insulated in a way that cannot yield a full and accurate accounting. The whole is viewed as simply the sum of its parts. Also, interactions among development projects produce both negative and positive effects that are screened and distorted in a narrow view. One project by itself may show virtues in the planning stage that are neutralized by the impacts of other projects built near or even far away. Or several projects may combine relatively minor negative effects into crisis proportions.

We are up to our armpits in shopping malls whose total effect is to cut the market pie ever smaller, drive up the cost of public subsidies, and eventually sap once successful local businesses. The number of projects explodes on us without an overall plan addressing the cumulative effects on traffic, schools, sewer and water, land use, and esthetics. Each proposal claims their pet project is inoffensive and innocuous, producing wonders to city and county and buckets of gold coins falling from the sky. Hardly a soul in government seems to be asking how this or that project fits into the overall matrix of development planning and impacts: How does it affect downtown or commuting or compact urban design goals? What of our precious water reserves? What is the real long-term subsidy cost to taxpayers? How does the project fit in to make a more balanced, better designed human community?

Instead, we are made to run a bizarre gauntlet. Today it's the Froom Ranch, the Dalidio property, Wal-Mart and Target, Santa Margarita and the Hearst Resort. Another week it's the airport expansion area, Albertson's market, the DeVaul project, the growing Broad Street commercial boom, or some 1,500 new homes on the water-starved

Nipomo Mesa. Each is seen as isolated from the other. Who can keep up with this explosive growth of super projects, megastores, and megasprawl, all fully automobile-dependent?

Every few months another big box store project is up for consideration and/or review. There is the Froom ranchland proposal at some 500,000 square feet off Los Osos Valley Road, the Madonna mall not far away, the Dalidio plan etc. There is the question of encroachment on urban reserve lines, while the county subtly claims that the city is dragging its feet on annexation of adjacent lands. The city council does not often talk about its own promotion of urban sprawl, and both city and county have eyes on the lure of sales tax dollars. It is the kind of shell game where the planning is segmented and often obscure.

The very language of environmental protection and good planning has been taken over, co-opted: "compact urban form"; "pedestrian orientation"; "sustainable growth"; "saving agricultural land"; "a downtown of human scale"; "quality of life". These terms are routinely bandied about to cover for projects and proposals mainly profit and debt producing, but inimical to the very values of environmental quality they should represent.

We have to end this charade of piecemeal planning, of acting as though there is something democratic and sacred about tearing apart a city or area and sinking it in the name of everyone's inherent right to do as they damn well please. Someone has to remind all concerned that it is both the city and county that have joint interests that must be defended for future generations. As the Supreme Court ruled more than 100 years ago, private property put to a public use acquires a public character and is subject to public regulation.

The city of San Luis Obispo is the jewel (self-tarnished, some would say) in the county's crown. We must learn to think in terms of master planning for a half-century or more, to cooperatively think through the needs of our city and region as a whole. All of us must learn to row together or be swamped together or separately. Without a cooperative effort at master planning involving government, the financial institutions, developers, and the public, we will end up with project-specific plan approvals based on highly technical environmental impact reports limited in scope and inherently myopic; SLO will look each year more and more like a sterile city in Sprawl County.

Businesses must come to fit into our local scale and economy. They must energize the economy rather than draw profits out, and thereby milk the local area for the advantage of powerful outside interests; these are willing and able to influence local elections in order to gain footholds, and eventually put any and every local enterprise at high risk. Developers need to be given guideposts and incentives to cooperate in sound planning. This also means competing against each other for approvals and permits based on much better design, smaller fit, and presentation of cooperative ventures that fully enhance the quality of life and environment. The public awaits that kind of honestly and imagination. Could we have an awakening on Los Osos Valley Road as a starter?

SOCIAL SCIENCE VIEWS EXCESSIVE GROWTH

What would social science say about growth and development plans for San Luis Obispo city and county? Would there be some guidance for the dispute over the plan for the fertile land known as both Dalidio and The Marketplace? And if there is instruction or caution to be gained from urban studies, why should anyone in government bother to care?

In democratic government, the populace has a voice, but decisions are usually left to elected representatives. Legally speaking, the duly constituted councils have as their choice to listen or not to listen to the testimony and opinion expressed. I remember telling the City Council that we urban specialists knew of two major ways to ruin a downtown: by building shopping malls on the periphery of the city and thereby sucking out the downtown shoppers; and second, by so catering to automobile garages in the downtown core as to choke the area in traffic and smog and cause people eventually to flee the area.

My advice must have been a big hit, because SLO's City Council soon adopted not one, but both of these tacks I had expressly warned against. Now we have to wait and see the eventual outcome, some of us taking solace in having given proper warning; others smiling ruefully with the late mountaineer and environmental leader, David Brower, and his caustic description of the senseless political pursuit of "strength through self-exhaustion."

That being said, here for the record are some conclusions of major studies of urban growth and development:

- The 1970 Stanford Land Use Study of San Jose sprawl is a classic. It concluded that city government policies "assured that development would take place not necessarily where the inhabitants as a whole wanted it nor where reason dictated, but where the developers chose to build." And developers most often chose to build where land could be obtained at the least expense, usually, in the case of San Jose, undeveloped areas substantially beyond the inhabited perimeters of the city. …Speculation was made profitable only through city cooperation in annexation, extension of sewers, storm drains, roads etc.

Karl Belser, San Jose County planning director wrote, "Along with the industries and new development came a water demand which overtaxed the underground supply ... As development proceeded, the very elements of amenity which made the area attractive in the first place were eroded away. Air pollution, land subsidence, increased flooding, impossible traffic congestion, airport noise and many other problems multiplied ad nauseam."

- A recent paper of the Rocky Mountain Institute in Colorado, focused on energy self-sufficiency and economic renewal, gives timely reason for concern. The authors, Michael Kinsley and L. Hunter Lovins find false the belief that an increased tax base relieves the tax burden and leads to improved public services. They quote a Minnesota study of three towns where agricultural land was subdivided. The result: It cost the local government more for necessary services than the gain from newly generated tax revenue. Further, used for farming, those lands generate "twice as much local tax revenue as it demands back in public services." This is backed by a study in Vermont, which concluded that those towns with the most taxable commercial and industrial property have, on average, higher general taxes on the inhabitants.

Why does this happen? Kinsley and Lovins conclude that part of the problem is that cities and counties do not provide for "rainy day" funds for capital replacement. Things wear out in normal use, but deterioration costs are not budgeted and banked by local government. In reality, our budgets are not balanced and current taxpayers are eventually stuck with back payments for deterioration as well as costs of borrowing money for questionable developments.

The authors conclude: "Many local government officials believe the only way out of the burden imposed by prior growth is to encourage new growth. They are trapped in this contradiction by the mental model that tells them they must grow to prosper. Once local governments begin to encourage expansion ... they are hooked on growth. There's no one to pay for the new infrastructure demanded by the new growth without yet another new round of expansion that, in turn, will also fail to pay for itself."

- But there are alternatives and some wise communities are beginning to turn things around. Plugging energy leaks (Osage, Iowa) and supporting existing community businesses are ways to stop unnecessary outflow of monies to outside interests such as chain stores. The idea is to increase the number of times dollars are spent within a community. "Oregon Marketplace" is a program that links local suppliers with local buyers, thus increasing jobs and community well-being. Avoiding depletion of local resources of land and quality of life is the key to sustainability.

Here, I can offer only a few examples of guidance from urban specialists. You, the reader, can ponder it or laugh it off, as you wish. The politicos will likely ignore it. They have their own agendas, sometimes known as "painting oneself into a corner." But whatever the case, please don't tell me that somehow San Luis Obispo is different and has little to learn from Minnesota or Oregon or Iowa or wherever. Having traveled the world, I know that it rains differently in Italy, Brazil, Africa, and New England. But however the rains comes down, you can bet on one thing for sure: Wherever you are, when it rains like hell, you are sure to get wet!

REVISE THE DOWNTOWN CONCEPT PLAN

Can a city delegate power for crucial decisions about city planning to a special interest group? Not ethically, and not if it desires wise control over its own destiny.

A recent City Council meeting revealed that the Downtown Association assumes, with some justification, it has been given a monopoly for physical planning within the central business area of our city. The DA is described as "a quasi-independent group controlled by business owners in our urban heartland." In this parochial view of downtown, the association is backed by city staff with whom it has special access.

Acting together, the two factions have promoted the costly Marsh Street garage expansion ($7 million - $10 million) and other pet projects and ideas included in the Downtown Concept Plan. The latter has no legal planning status and has never been subjected to a full public review, but serves as a front for expansionary projects promoted by the DA for using public money to push its own special interests. The "concept plan," widely exhibited in the form of a glossy diorama of a downtown San Luis Obispo of the future, contains 11 parking garages, surely enough to completely smother the city core in smog and snarled traffic. You would also be amazed at how the plan can quietly empty your pocketbook.

One progressive council member has wisely proposed the creation of a downtown task force that is much more representative of the public at large; also an audit of the DA's books and more control over the director of the DA, who is paid with city funds. Wider representation for all the interests of the people who use the downtown area would balance the lopsided influence of the DA and end the too cozy relationship that now exists between the association and City Hall. The downtown belongs to all of us. It has repeatedly been singled out for its pedestrian-friendly nature.

As the nerve center of our city, its aesthetics and its barter in ideas as well as goods should never be undervalued. While retail commerce is essential to the life-blood of a city, it should never be assumed the sole reason for a city center's existence. Visitors to SLO's downtown come for many reasons besides shopping. The government functions of the city and county alone account for a major share of the city's income; post office, courts and library are filled with visitors. There are various museums, art galleries and the San Luis Obispo Mission. Who can account the value of the Creek Walk as a place of conversation and repose, and a retreat for children at play? Thus, I was upset to hear a Chamber of Commerce staff member declare that where she grew up, people went downtown only to shop-- and that was good enough for her. How sad.

There is important work awaiting a truly representative downtown task force. The existing DA, largely made up of shopkeepers and business factions, pressures city staff and politicians to make planning decisions useful to its members' special interests but not necessarily healthy to city growth and balance. The DA ignores the counsel of locally aware citizens and university specialists in planning, who are much more aware of urban dynamics and transportation issues. The association hires outside consultants who are willing to tell it what it wants to hear. A new downtown task force must rescue San Luis Obispo from the twin ills that now afflict it- "garage-itis" and "mall-aria." Both attack the heart of the city, and both are fatal.

Why do mall planners lack the wisdom to build people-oriented centers with shopping attached, rather than the San Quentin-like parking lots surrounded by a stockade of insipid shops? The happy exceptions are the two downtown malls of Mr. Copeland, who was wise enough to get an architect who could see aspects beyond the cash register. The first such Downtown Mall shows a good variety of stores (perhaps too many of the chain variety) and movie theaters; it took the place of a huge empty lot that was too long seen as an ugly hole in the ground waiting for something to happen. Once built, it certainly spruced up and made dynamic the downtown core. It is always busy, and like its newer twin, some blocks away, is a fulcrum for downtown life.

Here are some vital needs to be addressed by a new downtown task force:

1. Development of a downtown pedestrian plan with teeth, a priority that should have been prerequisite to any planning decisions on parking, downtown access and transportation.

(That it does not yet exist is tribute to our fouled planning process.)

2. A complete revision of the Downtown Concept Plan, so that it is in accord with the best modern planning practice.

3. Redevelopment of the Downtown Access and Parking Plan so it is brought in line with the new pedestrian plan.

4. Reconsideration of all transportation funding and allocations to better alleviate traffic burdens.

5. Fitting multi-modal transportation funding into the total picture. In short, let's get our full community involved, and let's stop playing political games with SLO's future.

ABUNDANT VINEYARDS AND WINERIES
OF THE SAN LUIS OBISPO AREA

DEFENDING THE PUBLIC SECTOR

Until very recently, I had never thought too much about private vs. public sector employment. To me, creativity on the job is the important thing, and, having worked in both areas, I hardly gave a thought as to whether the paycheck was stamped with the name of a private business or that of a public agency. I never thought of it as a point of contention. On matters of employment, I drifted along like most people grumblingly content to live and let live.

But all that changed during a hike with some friends and a business acquaintance of theirs, with whom I soon crossed swords. We had been on trail for about 20 minutes when the talk turned to declining work opportunities and layoffs.

Mr. G., I shall call him, was delighted to declare his zest for the "Contract with America," seeing it as an opportunity to get rid of high-priced middle management and blue-collar slackers as well as useless government subsidies and public programs run by lazy and incompetent civil service bumblers. To Mr. G. only those people lacking in ambition and a work ethic would opt for the security of employment in the public sector, where lives are spent harassing the honest citizen who truly puts himself on the line. His words were spoken with sincerity and great emotion, and I answered him with equal, if barbed, honesty.

Mr. G., I hardly know you, and you seem to me a fine fellow out for a day's healthy exercise. Let me clear the air by fully introducing myself. I am one of those people who, for some 35 years, have been accepting public money for helping our young people, and many an adult like yourself, to get a better education. I see my job as one of sharpening critical thinking, of oiling rusty hinges so to speak, and thus opening doors to the world. I waved off his interruption. My students usually laugh, but sometimes groan under my intellectual expectations; so have those who have hired me as a consultant. But no one has ever accused me of being excessively security-conscious, shiftless, or bumbling. I would bet that you businessmen work as hard as I do, sometimes even on the golf course- but with entirely different rewards.

My newfound trail partner became at once apologetic. Mr. G., like so many unthinking people, was speaking of faceless public employees who make of public employment a refuge from the risks of life. He apologized and explained that he had perhaps overstated his case to make a point. Believe me, he declared, I really appreciate the job that is being done by exceptional people like you. I meant nothing personal.

But it is the very impersonality of your charge that disturbs me, I replied. While I understand what you do not MEAN to say, I am not at all sure that you realize what you are really saying. I fear you will continue in your conversations with others remembering all the bad experiences you may have had with public sector employees and none of the good. And you will conveniently forget the reasons for rules and regulations. Further, you have likely forgotten all the errors of management and slipshod work found also in the private sector. I don't want you to get away with that so easily.

I guess I went on the wrong hike, he smiled. I laughed.

No, this is the right hike if you want to clarify the nature of work and what constitutes a fair balance between the public and private sectors of the economy.

Work is work, he mused.

Yes, work is work, but what of reward and recognition? He agreed that such are not often parceled out fairly. But Mr. G. was just as quick to add that businessmen take far greater risks.

That they do, I nodded, but only if you think of risk mainly in monetary terms. How about the government scientist who risks years of effort on an experiment aimed at improving public health? The trash collector who risks a bad back? The paramedic or motorcycle cop riding the freeways? The librarian or teacher who drive themselves to bone-weariness trying to awaken an intellectual spark in apathetic students and their work-busy parents? Each of us risks in a different way. One person turns on by selling sports cars or loads of cement. Another likes to pilot a plane, a company or a social program. To still others it is the very thought of butterflies, composing music, or clean cities. It is this very mix of interdependent people and varied interests that yields national greatness.

Mr. G. agreed it was all very complicated and affirmed the importance of diversity. At that moment the time for debate was over. The sun shone strong and the trail turned sharply uphill. We focused on breathing clean ocean air and taking in mountain vistas protected by a public coastal commission. Later, we talked more … deeply, nicely.

I have thought about that exchange many times recently, as the full force of federal and state cutbacks begin to hit. From that day in the mountains, I date my resolve to fight back against unthinking criticism of public service. No more nice guy, hands off, soft-speaking from me. You want a fight, you'll get it. If you are one for cutting the public sector to the bone, then I am your adversary.

And I hope we'll meet soon. For if you really believe in downgrading environmental enforcement, turning off soft energy research, penny-pinching the schools, de-funding the libraries, cutting medical research, and turning the parks over to the commercial sector, you have not thought seriously about the future of this country.

However unwittingly, you see the public sector as an expense to the taxpayer rather than the investment it really is. You forget or never learned that public investment helped make our farmlands blossom, fueled much of our technological growth, and made our services and science among the best in the world. Too many of you carping critics extolling the private marketplace seem to forget that you graduated from publicly supported schools and colleges.

I know of failings in the public sector all too well. But let's apply the same measuring tape to balance scores. For I now record the errors and stupidities of the private realm and can reel off quite a few: Was there a ship built in two sections that did not fit when put together? Yes. It was built by a large private corporation on a cost-plus contract. It there a nuclear power plant built adjacent to an earthquake fault? You know it, thanks to the private power company.

Was the automobile market misread by American auto companies? Ask your neighbor as he parks his Toyota. Did private bank management succumb to a multi-billion dollar computer scam by one of its employees? Now we are talking about real greed. And who seems to regularly spill oil on our sand beaches? Not the publicly funded Coast Guard, you can bet on that.

And there are personal examples galore: having to wait in the flu ward for a simple travel shot, courtesy of a private health plan; a vapor lock problem misdiagnosed by several auto repair shops; my bank once refusing to accept the validity of my wife's signature on a check I brought in person, but which routinely accepted such if dropped anonymously in the night deposit. And so it goes. The airlines, the truckers, the farmers, the corporations- all screwing up, and most feeding at the public trough. There's the real estate lobby, the insurance lobby, the tobacco lobby, the political PACs, the defense contractors, the AMA, and the lawyers, all screaming about the virtues of free enterprise, while cleverly grubbing for tax loopholes and special treatment by the government. Yes, let's talk about corporate welfare for a change!

And do the companies that are so delighted to lay off tens of thousands of workers ever wonder who in America will be able to buy their products in the future? I doubt it, for that would take real thinking and a concern for our collective future as a nation.

So when you next feel like finding a public scapegoat, do remember me. I've studied up and, boy, am I ready. To my friends in the private sector ... Greetings!

IV: POPULATION, LAND AND THE QUALITY OF LIFE

HOW MUCH SHOULD WE WORRY ABOUT GROWTH?

Crossing the Atlantic Ocean for the first time, the president of a large agricultural college gazed at the endless expanse of water and sadly remarked, "Too bad we can't plant it all in alfalfa." One sees what one thinks about most of the time. Finding open land many a developer sees only buildings and profit and would likely "plant it all" edge to edge. We tend to think that it can't happen here – or can it? The San Luis Obispo General Plan allows for slow growth to 57,700 population by 2022. Yet, according to the Packard Foundation, population on the Central Coast of California is expected to balloon by 175 percent over the next ten years. Given the burst of development locally –malls, tracts, shopping centers, freeway expansion etc. – is it realistic to think that SLO is either willing or able to constrain growth in keeping with environmental limits and amenities? Can we buck the trend?

I returned from a visit to the Palm Desert area, where the mania for growth has taken precedence over environmental balance. I observed that from Palm Springs to Indio, easy access to the mountains and desert floor is no longer common. In many areas, it is barely possible to find an open path into the hills and canyons that so long attracted visitors. Access roads and paths are often now gated and guarded. The once dry natural landscape is carpeted with lush lawns and an enormous sprawl of shopping centers and walled condominium complexes. Fortunes have been made selling locking gates and concrete block at uncountable cost to the legendary freedom to roam the desert. As the urbanized expanse continues to grow, the "desert" looks more and more like everywhere else.

In twenty years the area has grown to more than 130,000 residents. Some eighty golf courses in the Palm Springs-Palm Desert area are daily irrigated, including one wholly owned and restricted for personal use by a billionaire. Artificial lakes and waterfalls dot the fancy hotels and country clubs. I asked a local realtor the source for all the water. "Don't worry," he replied, "We have the largest aquifer in California and it's replenished from the Colorado River." When I explained how precariously dependent that is on growth demands of Arizona and Nevada, he chuckled, "If we don't get another drop of water from there, we still have a twenty year supply."

Twenty years. A time frame for those who live in a futureless society. You see, it CAN happen here. Talk to a Palm Springs hairdresser, who fled her Oceanside home before a wave of development that turned her commute into a nightmare, and her area into an ugly sprawl. "So I came here, and now what? The same is happening all over again. People walling themselves off, getting richer by controlling the land and ruining the desert for the rest of us and our kids... Scary scenario, much anger.

And the kids? I found very few on the remaining open trails. But the shopping malls are loaded with them, the "mall rats" so-called, learning the pattern of spending leisure time buying and ogling things and each other. They are blasé about exploring the desert they live in, or came to visit with their parents. In an era when "fun" is more likely measured in dollars expended, in dune buggy thrills, the desert itself is viewed as boring.

We forget how much mall culture infects lifestyle and values, how it adversely affects perception of nature. Why go to the desert if, aside from climate, it is a clone of what one finds almost everywhere in our cities? Why travel to San Luis if it becomes submerged in the very same pattern of rampant growth that will ruin its unique identity? Too few people ask these questions, including some who parade as advocates of "reasonable growth". Sustainability is one valid measure of reasonableness. Projects already approved or pending on the central coast, for example, put at risk our water resources.

We hear much about "outside money" and are urged to have faith in local developers. We're told that they know the lay of the land and have a sense of vision and stewardship. Some do, but it is a rare combination, and often skewed by the temptations of profit. There's tons of money to be made in open spaces in San Luis and elsewhere. And we've heard the familiar phrase: "When they say it is not about money ... face it, it's about money!" Most development dollars are blended from various sources. Faith in local control of greed is likely blind. Let the buyer beware.

"Don't worry," a member of our Planning Commission answered me. "Less than five percent of SLO County land is urbanized." Well, less than one-tenth of one percent of Nevada is urbanized, but I have no desire to live in Reno or Las Vegas.

Population growth and sprawl accelerate with surprising speed. Look around. View the plans down the road. Count the bulldozers. Should you be worried that it can happen here? You bet. Because it's happening.

COUNTY GROWTH PROJECTIONS HAVE LIMITS

The Tribune series on future growth of San Luis Obispo county performed a valuable public service. The focus on the Solimar study projecting 100,000 new residents by 2023 at most, brought a very tame public reaction compared to the outcries over the state mandate for some 17,000 new homes by 2009. Most people apparently assume, even reluctantly, that 100,000 new residents in the next twenty years is more or less inevitable. Where they all will live is another story.

Let us not forget that after 2023 there will be 2024. The acceptance now of the 100,000 figure as reasonable means that between 2024 and 2044 we are likely setting the stage for accelerated growth to as many as 350,000 new residents. Fast growth builds its own momentum (San Jose, the San Fernando Valley, Orange County) as semi-rural areas with small urban cores, such as our own, are suddenly drowned by a flood of migrants and an exploding local population.

Population projections can be used to justify current trends and future growth patterns that need not happen. There is nothing authentic in the 100,00 estimate- or any other. In effect, projections become reality by inducing governments to make major investments in sewage plants, roads, water supplies and schools, which then parlay into population growth. But current trends might be only a temporary aberration. Migration patterns and fertility rates change due to economic and social conditions.

Trends are not fixed in stone, and school enrollments or employment also might increase or decrease because of a variety of factors. It is bad planning to use growth projections that cater to special interests, which are largely unconcerned with long-run environmental consequences or bonded indebtedness of taxpayers. Yet, it's a well known facet of local politics. The higher the projection, the more the fast-growth lobbies rub their hands in glee. More inhabitants is not necessarily better, and may well create worse conditions- a concept lost on city public relations efforts. And towns love to exaggerate their needs in the hopes of attracting more grants and dollars.

Surely, growth is going to occur in SLO county. Whether this means 40,000, 80,000, 100,000, or 250 thousand added population in the next 20-40 years is a matter of conjecture, not scientific prediction;

there are too many variables for that. But how then can we best prepare for and manage population increase?

All of the sensible choices aim at protection against sprawl, guarding greenbelt and prime farmland, protecting our water supplies and environment, building affordable housing, and keeping development within urban reserve lines. Population projection thus must reflect these goals, not simply project current trends. All local projections of growth should add up and equal the California state projection, and all state projections should equal the national projection of the Census Bureau and the Environmental Protection Agency. Otherwise "booster politics" rules.

These goals have startling implications in the post-9/11 era. For example, national energy policy dictates that sprawl be stopped so that heavy dependence on commuting and oil-use comes under control. Agricultural policy and land use laws will have to change to protect prime farmland in order to feed a growing population. Cities will have to change codes and invest in high-rise housing to save energy. And there is need to reduce infrastructure costs (sewers, roads etc) associated with sprawl and allow workers and professionals to live economically.

High rises need not be ugly and jammed, the bugaboo of housing. Above all, they need to be aesthetically planned: architecturally pleasing with green space and mixed housing. There are ample examples already built in the United States and abroad.

There will always be objections to reforming business as usual. But the population-explosion genie is out of the bottle- and politicians are trying to hide from it. The future is already here and we either seize the moment and ensure good planning or continue to waste our treasury by hyping the wonders of growth and pretending things are under control.

MORRO BAY ESTUARY AT LOW TIDE

MORRO ROCK AND BAY FROM BLACK HILL

SOLVING OUR HOUSING CRUNCH

The statewide deficit in middle and lower income affordable homes is alarming. Our fast-growing California population leads the state to insist that SLO county take a fair share of the load by planning for at least 18,900 new homes over the next six years.

Our local politicos insist that even 10,000 new homes in seven years is unrealistic. But the overloaded big cities can no longer sustain the lion's share burden of rampant growth. Worse, population, immigration and family planning are seen in many quarters as either heresy or political dynamite.

Solutions to the housing crisis, however, do exist if we are willing to expand our horizons. Already, we have seen notice of a move in Paso Robles to allow housing to be built over stores in commercial areas. San Luis also is beginning to do the same. Many cities have instituted this kind of zoning reform for over 50 years with no degradation in quality of life. Indeed, as the price of housing has skyrocketed in California and elsewhere in the U.S., the middle-class dream of home ownership has all but vanished; revival is a fading hope weighed down by archaic building and land use codes, head-in-the-sand planning, and futile crisis politics.

The next generation of buyers (and renters) will be in even worse shape. The nationwide economic collapse has thrown all the housing cards up in the air. Do we go back to primogeniture (property rights of the firstborn) or do we move ahead to a new vista for housing? Just when will the housing sector revive? And to what extent? Frankly, no one really knows.

Assuming a healthy economic revival, view the Airport Expansion and Margarita Area, which runs roughly from Tank Farm Road to Orcutt Rd to Bullocks Lane and the Amtrak rail line. Master-planned, they could easily house 9000 people, but not as it is now envisioned. With wiser planning and all 13 property owners involved, the Orcutt Area might hold about 700 residences, a big park and a neighborhood store. Further, large portion of the Airport expansion and Margarita properties could be devoted to open space surrounding Righetti Hill and several creeks. Expanded housing would consist of high-rise apartments adjacent to condos and town-homes, plus a sprinkle of single-family housing.

A real mix, that is. And not segregated sections by housing type It would be akin to highly successful Columbia, Maryland, and the renewal effort in Atlanta known as "Atlantic Station." Both cities are planned for high quality of life. Rapid transit and an inter-village minibus system, affordable rentals, energy efficiency, esthetics, and social facets of city living are major aspects of the Columbia design. For example, children walk to school without having to cross heavily trafficked streets. (Businesses poured in because they found a beautiful, safe, and friendly environment for employees and operations.)

Atlantic Station, by comparison, is just breaking ground in an effort to create a pedestrian-friendly atmosphere of mixed commercial-residential in a now dilapidated area of downtown. What Atlanta is doing in the heat of desperation over sprawl and traffic jams, San Luis could be doing as a cool preventative!

The housing mix with well-designed green-space proved irresistible to buyers and renters, the opposite of most predictions. It is a real alternative to development carpeting the land. Now extend the analogy to the whole of San Luis, where the single family home dominates. It's the dinosaur of our times (I live in one) but still almost the only option. The land policies cater to people who thirst after huge square footage as a symbol of "success"- part of the "bigger must be better" delusion, and a contorted psychology brought to the housing market in an era of environmental limits. Especially for retirees, I must say it is a bit too late for chasing castles in the sky.

The city and county could change zoning laws and offer tax advantages to duplex and triplex homes that would offer opportunity for small entrepreneurs, and reasonable housing and costs to thousands now shoved off the market. Yes, it will make the city denser, but with strong architectural, landscape and esthetic standards also more attractive. The key is to support housing starts that do good for the community both in terms of beauty and rental or purchase possibilities. No more housing such as we have in high-rent shacks, high-rise "prisons", energy-inefficient "ranchettes" (with their demand for roads and city services) or a monoculture of look-alike and boring tracts. The fly in the ointment is not lack of governmental ability, but a backward mindset ... and ultimately a limited fresh water supply!

Today, it still pays for the developer to submit designs for huge houses that only a few can afford, compounding the housing crisis for the city and county. (Permit applications for affordable housing seldom reach planning commission tables.) Because of the lack of diversity of housing, the single-family home has become a principal cause of urban sprawl in the county and an expensive consumer of urban services. In fact, it is "subsidy for the wealthy," prompted and enforced by housing codes and incentives completely outdated by modern reality. The fast-growth genie is out of the bottle and we are headed toward boundless sprawl by not facing the real challenge of compact urban form. Personally, I might wish for other alternatives, but I see no future in fooling ourselves. Perhaps my readers can offer an alternative scenario that works, rather than simply bewailing green alternatives that face up to realities. Let's give the poor consumer and the middle class person a break for a change by designing with population pressures in mind- even if we can't seem to otherwise rationally address them.

PRAISE FOR HOUSING SERIES

To the Editor:

The Tribune's series on housing was top-rate. It was well-balanced, incisive, and generally well-written. Of course, you are going to get complaints from readers who cannot see beyond their noses and who do not appreciate articles that force them to think. It's almost as if people don't want to realize the damage they are doing to the next generation by clinging to a housing pattern that evolved before the age of urbanism and intense population pressure.

Never mind. You have opened the door to the choices that will engender the future of San Luis Obispo city and county. The important step now is to get the opinion leaders and the politicians (not necessarily the same thing) to explore what other areas and cities have done to stop costly urban sprawl and so help bring about an effective and productive living pattern for our urbanizing community. It's not good enough to say it won't happen here. It will happen here and the body that will pay for the ignorance is your child's.

Let's get more examples from around the country, on par with your Berkeley profile. Interview the generators of change and let us readers learn how they measure their success and how they overcame resistance to change. It can be done and in a way that is fair and just. *-Ira Winn, Professor of Urban Studies (Emeritus)*

FARMLAND STATISTICS DEMAND CLOSER LOOK

A recent U.S. Census Bureau report found that San Luis Obispo country has 13 percent more farmland than it had in 1900. While some take comfort in this statistic, we have to look behind the raw data to obtain a full picture.

As urbanites have pushed into traditional farmlands, and urban sprawl has become a signature of our times, more and more marginal land is being put into production. The measure of agricultural land and output cannot be taken solely in terms of acreage lost or gained, but more accurately in the kind of land that has been taken out of production.

It is *prime* farmland, not simply any land that can be planted that is the key to the puzzle. A thousand new acres of lesser-quality land opened up in the great plains, for example, cannot equal in productive value 100 acres of vastly more fertile land in, say, San Luis Obispo or Santa Barbara counties.

For one thing, the growing season is almost all year, and for another, the vastly richer soils here and the warmer climate allow for a wide variety of crops, such that 80 percent of all the table vegetables available in the U.S. come from California. Yet, some partisans of "property rights" insist, even in the face of a greatly expanding population, that ag land depletion can't happen here.

How wrong they are can be seen by what happened in the Santa Clara Valley (San Jose area), which, in 1946 had a population the same as SLO city today. With roughly 60,000 city people, it was both county seat and center for the food processing industry for more than 100,000 acres of orchards and vegetable crops that made up that county's agricultural base. San Jose then was one of the 15 most productive agricultural counties in the U.S.

However, as then planning director Karl Belser later explained, in 1950 San Jose "came under a new aggressive administration, which made no bones about its goal of making San Jose the Los Angles of the North. It formulated definite goals for expansion and growth … and the city moved with alacrity to implement them. Over the next 20 years, the entire area became urbanized as some farmers took quick advantage of the speculative wave in land values, while many were forced eventually to flee because of rising taxes for urban services and the chaotic pattern of sprawl, which caused endless problems.

Today, government officials and developers are much more shifty about their intent, often hiding behind catch phrases such as "mitigation of negative impacts," "modern growth," "supply and demand," "the primary needs of an automobile-centered era," etc. But as a Stanford University study concluded by 1970, "San Jose shows what can happen when an aggressive city or county government is responsible to only a narrow constituency and is dedicated to short-sighted goals." In 25 years, the Santa Clara Valley had added well over a half-million people! Go there and see the rest of the story. And that is why the SOAR (land use controls) initiatives are so critical now, before the San Jose wave picks up even more steam here in San Luis Obispo.

American Farmland Trust, committed to stopping the loss of productive farmland and to promoting ecologically sensitive farm practices, has spotlighted 20 regions of the United States as especially threatened areas. These include the great Sacramento and San Joaquin valleys of Central California. Twenty-one percent of the nation's loss of prime farmland occurred in these regions between 1982-1992. AFT finds that suburban sprawl is also causing inefficient use of land, roads, and other infrastructure, creating serious traffic congestion and air pollution, and limiting future U.S. options to deal with social, economic, and food insecurity problems. At current rates of land conversion, there will be 13 percent fewer acres of high quality farmland to produce food, while the U.S. population will be almost doubling to nearly 400 million people.

A U.S. Department of Agriculture survey found that in the 10 years 1982-1992, cropland decreased 9 percent, developed land increased by 18 percent and rangeland decreased by 2.4 percent. The increase in developed land came from conversion of 5.4 million acres of forest land, 4 million acres of cropland, 2.5 million acres of pastureland, and some 2 million acres of rangeland.

American Farmland Trust advocates a revision of Federal and state laws, including real estate taxation, to help keep agricultural land in the hands of farm families committed to continued and sound farming. On a parallel track, the SOAR initiatives seek to put zoning changes in the hands of the citizenry of SLO city and county and out of the hands of politicians who have proven open and beholden to lobbying pressure. If you don't think these steps are vital for long-term food security in the United States, I suggest you sit down and figure how many truckloads of oranges, tomatoes, grapes, peppers, strawberries, and avocados you can expect to grow and ship from say Wyoming or New Hampshire.

Note: The SOAR initiative was defeated by county voters.

WINE GRAPES IN SLO'S ROLLING COUNTRYSIDE

SATURDAY FARMER'S MARKET IN SLO

LET'S BE WARY OF THE COST-BENEFIT ANALYSIS GAME

If the currents of anti-environmentalism holds sway, practically every act of government and every enforcement action affecting the economy will be held hostage to cost-benefit analysis.

On the surface, it seems only a reasonable and proper requirement that government agencies and the Congress itself approve, and the executive branch enforce only those laws and regulations that have been extra-carefully weighed as to their impact on the economy and employment. In the deregulatory climate current, it is viewed as only fair that environmental and health regulations be judged in terms of their "real costs" to society as well as their ecological benefits.

But what does cost-benefit really mean in terms of long-range protection of public and environmental health and safety? What will be the effect on such as toxic waste, endangered species, the wilderness, etc.?

A simple forestry example reveals the complexity: To the developer, the XYZ forest is easily weighed in terms of board feet of lumber; to the exporter, it is raw logs to be sold to Japan. To the fisherman, however, XYZ is a protective cover that filters and cleans the flowing river or stream, a resource that can easily be silted with waste and runoff from logged and eroded land.

To the recreationist, this wild land and its beautiful trees are a refuge from the crowded and polluted city. And to the wildlife biologist, the mature forest particularly is a home and haven, a nesting site, a feeding ground, and a protective cover from potential and real predators, animal and human.

Given the widely different and contradictory nature of these perspectives, how will cost-benefit analysis solve the problem of what to do or not do with the XYZ forest?

The answer, it appears, is to assign a numerical value to each potential use or action, costs on one side of the ledger and benefits on the other. Perhaps this will be done by a panel of scientific experts, perhaps by a citizen's committee chosen for their sagacity and/or political influence.

No matter. The history of such efforts is one of stalemate, under-the-table dealing, and stormy outcry. The history of philosopher-kings is one more of kings than of philosophers. At any rate, no one extolling the cost-benefit approach is able to say with certainty how this new attempt would work, or work better than before cost-benefit is implemented.

But one can be sure that a majority vote will constitute a "democratic decision." Unfortunately, in the world of ecology, with its synergistic and long range reactions, nature bats last and holds trump card even in the face of democratic votes. One is reminded of pollster Lindsay Rogers' acute observation that polling (like plumbing the collective mind of experts) is a means of being precise about matters of which we will remain ignorant.

Instead of solving environmental and health problems, the cost-benefit avenue quickly turns into a blind alley. It stalemates government preventative and enforcement action protective of nature's balance and public health and safety; it opens the door to endless and costly litigation.

Perhaps cost-benefit does help employment, by fielding an army of "experts" self-styled and real, while throwing the entire regulatory apparatus into neutral and reverse-- the real aim of some cost-benefit schemers. The end result is a deadly game of gridlock under the guise of fair play and "a sound economy." The big losers will be the American public, already swindled umpteen times over, and the next generation, which will have to pay for it all.

Also paying dearly will be the flora and fauna, which lack standing in the courts; lost in the cost-benefit accounting will be their full value and legitimate claims to life, liberty, and the right to be left alone. What it all comes down to is that decisions on life and sustainability of the global and local environments are really value questions that cannot be reduced to and do not lend themselves to simplistic and mechanical schemes and models.

Some years ago, I sat in as consultant on an Environmental Protection Service lecture in Jerusalem on the "virtues" of the cost-benefit approach. The presenter was an American professor who argued that even the most difficult of decisions could readily be reduced to a numerical balance sheet that would be both objective and fair.

To illustrate, he utilized the question of whether it would be right to shoot the last pair of ducks of a given species left on Earth. On one side of the blackboard, he assigned numbers for all the virtues of saving them; on the other side, he put the numbers for hunting them by a mythical hungry tribe. As I remember it, the totals came pretty close to even. Just before he was going to play King Solomon, someone in the audience shouted that it was all fine and dandy for the hungry people to do the figuring, and even for the American professor to play with the adding machine. But who exactly, he demanded, would assign numbers for the population yet unborn, who had not yet even heard of these ducks or had a chance to see their wild beauty? And who would assign numbers from the viewpoint of the ducks?

Our poor professor managed a wan smile, and, in Chekhov's phrase in his story, "The Cherry Orchard", faded away " as a dying duck in a thunderstorm."

THE FOLLY OF "DEMOCRATIC" BUILDING HEIGHT LIMITS

When jokingly asked how long a man's legs should be, lanky President Abraham Lincoln retorted, "Just long enough to reach the ground." Current arguments over the proper height limit for tall buildings in San Luis Obispo might benefit from Lincoln's waggish insight.

There is no quick and simple answer to this central city question because an answer for one building or area might not be a healthy solution for another nearby. "Tall" is not only in the eye of the beholder but in the sight of the mountain and the skyline, in the shadow cast, and in the beauty or ugliness the architecture presents.

As a city spreads geographically, it imposes significant burdens on itself and on surrounding communities. Many of the handicaps of a dispersed city are hidden from the casual observer: longer commutes, intensifying energy costs, taxes to pay for sewers, roads, police and fire, and education- burdens often thrown off on adjacent or suburban communities where housing costs are less. Thus, rural land gets gobbled up and farmland is paved over and lost to the productive potential of the state and region.

From another perspective, the compact high-rise city can become a beehive of business activity but without an aesthetic heart to keep alive the psychological and spiritual drives of a vibrant city culture- a marketplace for learning and the exchange of ideas in an aesthetically compatible setting. Without these positives, the city center deteriorates in time and eventually decays into a plastic form, like so many towns that have traded away the uniqueness of their marketplace for a dull, carbon-copy golden calf.

So what is the desirable height limit for buildings in downtown San Luis Obispo? 38 feet? 56 feet? Perhaps 75 feet? It's the wrong kind of question! To put the issue in that context makes no more sense than insisting that all pants should measure the same leg length. The proper height for downtown buildings is a function of a number of variables including the shadow cast, the closeness to other high-rises, the height of the land on which a given building sits, the blockage of views, wind tunnel and traffic effects, etc. To establish a rule for an entire downtown or urban area is the height of folly.

A building, for example, on the higher ground of Palm Street requires a different measure than on the lower ground of Marsh Street. And thus we can be happy with the Copeland decision to cut the height of the Chinatown project.

There are novel ways to move around the problem of finding a universal height limit. One would be to draw sector or zone lines on a map of downtown, dividing the city into quarter-mile squares. The city could then create fixed standards allowing only one building of more than four stories in each sector. A variation of this principle would have developers compete for "tall building permits" based on the projected shadow, energy conservation, and aesthetic-architectural judgments by a professional panel. Still another approach would involve a lottery for tall building "rights". The merit of any lottery is that it is equally fair or equally unfair to all parties involved and eliminates the possibility of payoffs and political shenanigans.

Although citizens express differing points of view about large projects proposed or in process, the public would still like to keep San Luis Obispo a distinctive California town with a unique ambiance and a balanced and healthy market-place. Smallness of scale is not a virtue to be ignored. There are more and better ways to reach for the sky than to open the floodgates to unbalanced growth that can wreak havoc, especially in tougher economic times.

One height rule for all might sound democratic, but it bears the seeds of crowded and unimaginative development. In approaching the strong points of a more compact city, we must not throw away what we all enjoy about our environment. It's another good example of why planning must venture to think outside the box.

V. ENERGY ISSUES AND RISKS IN SLO COUNTY & BEYOND

RADIATION WITHOUT REPRESENTATION IS TYRANNY

The American struggle for national legitimacy began under the banner, "Taxation Without Representation Is Tyranny." Radiation without effective representation is no less a modern tyranny, even more so because the consequences are so harmful to biological life and our legacy to future generations.

We look around us and see a virtual national epidemic of cancer. Some people wonder if there is any connection to areas harboring operating nuclear power plants.

Studies of strontium absorption in baby teeth indicate some intake of this element in place of calcium in growing bone. Strontium-90, with a half-life of 28 years, is a byproduct of nuclear generation and is cancer producing.

One controversial study of eight geographical areas with closed nuclear power plants showed a significant drop in local infant deaths and in childhood cancer rates within two years of shutdown, especially in downwind counties. By contrast, areas within 100 miles of operating nuclear plants, especially downwind, showed strong cancer patterns.

These findings have been rebutted by the nuclear industry, which is shielded from making definitive cancer studies or releasing full data that normally would be required for any meaningful health study. So far, no one can be certain of the degree of hazard.

Today, it is hard to find a family that is not aware of someone affected by cancer, although the cause or causes of the deadly disease may not be readily traceable for a given person. Pesticides, natural background radiation from the sun, food additives and a host of new chemicals and biological agents poured into the environment daily are all strongly suspect, along with the added question of radiation from the generation of nuclear power. All these factors add to any genetic burden.

Every representative body and every thinking citizen must become aware of dangers posed by environmental toxins and by the local issues of radioactive waste storage and transport. The lack of certainty is not a valid reason for relaxing concern or not pressing ahead with more rigorous investigation.

More than 80,000 synthetic chemicals are in use in the United States, and the number is rapidly growing. More than 90 percent of these have never been tested for possible effects on human health. Some accumulate in body fat, and many are extremely difficult to neutralize once put into the environment.

Nuclear radiation -odorless, colorless, and tasteless-can cause a health crisis that affects everyone, those aware of it as well as people unaware or unconcerned.

Our County Board of Supervisors voted 3 to 2 against adopting intervener status before the Nuclear Regulatory Commission. Why they voted so is a topic of controversy and surmise; the vote negatively affects forthcoming hearings on added storage above ground of radioactive waste at Diablo Canyon. The public, unlike elected officials, is limited to making comments at such hearings in 3-minute time slots and is never assured of getting full and candid disclosure. The supervisors can exert real power, if they so choose.

The County Board of Supervisors is a key lifeline in defense of the health and safety of the public. Local government action is the best way of assuring some degree of local control. As President Eisenhower explained after five frustrating years attempting to limit federal program expansion, "In each instance, state inaction or inadequate action has forced emergency federal action."

Even federal attention is no guarantee of wise programming. Sometimes the federal NRC becomes a captive of the very nuclear industry it is supposed to regulate in the public interest. The public needs forthright answers to questions about the degree of cancer among nuclear workers in our county, and this information should be tied to a baseline health study that plots cancer clusters, if any, in the SLO area.

Perhaps no one can yet say definitively that nuclear generation is a prime cause of rise in cancer rates, but smoking guns do raise serious questions that demand probing. No sacred cows can be allowed in the search for answers, and our local government must awaken to the challenge. Let's have no unasked or unanswered questions. Leaving to future generations the burden of handling our radioactive waste is both a moral and technical default.

Radiation with unenthusiastic representation is sickening. Radiation without representation is tyranny!

STANDING ON THE SIDE OF SAFETY

In calling for local government to candidly question the nuclear industry and to support baseline health studies of cancer patterns in SLO county, I have obviously touched a raw nerve, as seen in Diablo's rebuttal.

I was very careful to put low-level radiation from nuclear power plants as but one of a number of suspected causes of cancer, including background radiation from the sun, pesticides, food additives, and a host of new chemical and biological agents daily poured into the environment. The vitriol of the rebuttal ("sensational statements, junk science" etc.) is typical in the history of nuclear industry defensiveness. What the rebuttal essentially concludes is that the nuclear industry is "fail-safe", 100% clean, and is responsible for no cancer at all.

In matters of public health and safety, the citizenry must maintain a skeptical stance. The history of nuclear power in the U.S. contains, unfortunately, a pattern of blackballed, distinguished scientists and critics, whose findings on radiation and exposure do not go along with the prevailing industry line. As a long time reader of the Bulletin of the Atomic Scientist, I am aware of that. It becomes almost impossible for scientists outside the nuclear industry establishment and its privileged contractors to gain access to data that would provide a clear and definitive view of the relationship between nuclear power and cancer. Every industry has its share of dangers and accidents. But nuclear radiation is not just cumulative; it has genetic implications beyond this generation. And the industry continues to lose credibility by its stonewalling behind "privileged doctor-patient relationships" that supposedly allow no public disclosure of cancers among workers at nuclear power plants.

In 1995, the NRC eliminated the mandate to assess health effects of radiation emissions, when considering extensions and re-licensing of nuclear power plants.

And a move is on to lower radiation exposure standards. If the industry really wishes to gain public trust, it would be better served by opening up medical data (no names need be given) on workers at Diablo (and other nuclear power plants) who have experienced cancer. These results could then be plotted on a countywide grid, and tied to an overall baseline health study. Then we could end the game of "my quoted study is better than your quoted study." The NRC stance in Washington is to make it harder and harder for scientists and citizens to question the nuclear line. Where secrecy rules, anything deceptive is possible. And the history of science is filled with so-called "fail-safe" conclusions, as well as gross and harmful deception. I would hope that the rebuttal writer is correct, and that low-level radiation from nuclear power plants eventually proves completely contained. But for the while, I'll look with a dubious eye.

--Not Published

HEADLANDS AT MONTANA DE ORO, LOOKING SOUTH
TOWARD DIABLO CANYON NUCLEAR PLANT.

REMARKS TO THE ATOMIC SAFETY AND LICENSING BOARD, NRC, ON THE UTILITY (PG&E) PROPOSAL TO INCREASE STORAGE OF SPENT FUEL AT THE DIABLO CANYON NUCLEAR POWER PLANT SITE

March 24, 2003:

I speak as a citizen of San Luis Obispo city and county. Today, I choose to focus on unanticipated events that could affect or have affected nuclear power plants, and the unanticipated consequences thereof.

As I understand it, the utility proposes to increase its storage of spent fuel assemblies from approximately 2000 at present to 4400 in the near future. In 50 years time, each and every radioactive assembly would degrade from over two million curies to about 100,000 curies- or from a surface dose rate of 200,000 rems per hour to about 8,000 rems per hour over a period of fifty years. The problem is that 500 rems per hour is lethal to humans as well as animal and much plant life. The kill power of such an amount of radiation is enormous and really not well understood by many people. It is far more in quantity and potential danger than the total amount of radiation released at Hiroshima.

In 2009 and 2010, multiple leaks of radioactive tritium (12.3 year half-life and the capability of traveling long distances) have been discovered at the 38 year-old Vermont Yankee nuclear power plant. Inaccurate testimony by plant owners covering up the situation has now led to a move by state government to shut down the entire facility.

We residents of central coastal California are being asked to leave safety questions to the "experts." The history of modern technology is fraught with failures that the so-called experts did not anticipate or could not control. Indeed, the real "experts" in this situation are the people of the California coast who live here and who will have to bear the consequences of any release of radiation whether caused by human error, mechanical breakdown, or natural disaster.

It is as if a giant radioactive land mine has been implanted on the California coast, and now we are being asked to double the danger. We are being told that it is all under control and that virtual fail-safe conditions exist. "Fail-safe" is a convenient but totally arbitrary and theoretical construct which works fine and holds true until it runs into the complicated workings of practical reality and human error... however long that might take to occur.

These are recorded as unanticipated events, the focus of my presentation. In looking over some of the history of atomic energy incidents, I easily found a cogent example. It took place at Indian Point, New York in the 1970's- not so very long ago in terms of geologic time and the life of radioactive isotopes which can stay in the environment and kill for 50 or 100 or even thousands of years in some cases.

Attempts at in-place repair of steam generators at Indian Point (New York) was foiled by high radiation fields that restricted worker repair time to a total of 20 minutes, including 10 minutes to crawl into and out of the hole. Defective tubing had to be cut out and repaired offsite, and reinsertion for those workers was not possible because they had reached the limit of radiation exposure. Almost every union welder in New York City, many without nuclear experience, had to be rotated in to finish the job.

A second radiation outage involved radioactive piping. It took eight months and all of Con Edison's skilled welders plus 50 health physicists to monitor exposure and about 600 personnel in all. A similar outage at a non-nuclear plant would take two weeks and about 25 workers. A more recent worrisome incident occurred at the Davis-Besse Nuclear Power Plant in Ohio. Only a few years ago, its reactor head almost burst because of equipment failure and leaky welds which were not repaired in a timely fashion. Why? Because of management and the NRC's desire to keep the plant producing power.

This brings us to an important point with respect to Diablo Canyon. With wet or dry storage, the degree of radiation danger will be far greater. There is no containment dome for the spent fuel pools. Where will the experienced personnel come from and be available to work close-in with a huge radiation emergency? How will they create some degree of shutdown or control?

Frankly, in such circumstances there is no easy long run control possible. In an emergency with spent fuel pools, there is no escape, no exit, and no return to a radiation saturated area. We are betting the lives and economic livelihood of the people of California and future generations on a twin gamble: 1) nothing devastating will go wrong for hundreds or even thousands of years; and 2) human error never has to be factored in, despite past experience. To accept such a gamble is the ultimate in hubris-- human arrogance and overweening pride and self-confidence. "Whom the gods destroy, they first make mad."

I have two recommendations for the Nuclear Regulatory Commission: It is your responsibility, not just that of concerned citizens, to warn communities of the nature of the gamble. You must explain that there are no technical fixes waiting in the wings, and thus in the event of a failure there is no exit and no easy or prompt return to irradiated lands. Honesty and candor is your best policy.

Second, and regardless of your decision, I would like you to post a plaque made of some long-lived material with the names of all those who make the decision on spent fuel assembly storage. We have had enough of faceless bureaucracies. It is only fair and proper that future generations should know who is responsible for such momentous decisions.

I wish you courage and compassion in reflecting on these portentous issues. I thank you for your attention. --- Ira Winn

BIGGEST ENVIRONMENTAL BLUNDERS
IN JUST ONE SAMPLE YEAR

When the September moon looms in the night sky, it is time to assess environmental lunacies for the year gone by. This is the first such competition. Let's begin with a mix of wry humor and deadly seriousness. It's a wake-up call, and a lot more sober than an "ugly man" contest.

Practically everyone claims to be enraptured by the environment. And yet, given the defects of humankind - selfishness, shortsightedness, avarice, prejudice, over-competitiveness, and egomania-- it is only just and proper that the worst be spotlighted. Perhaps the biggest question is why politicians and planners are so prone to blunder, to get lost in blind alleys, and to make decisions inimical to their professed goals?

We must learn more quickly to recognize human frailty and foolishness that yield long-run planetary pain and despoilation of the environment. You may compile your own list, but here are my picks for environmental lunacies in twelve months 1996-1997:

An "invincible ignorance" award to a generation of managers of the Hanford nuclear reservation in eastern Washington state. For years, they have stubbornly maintained that heavy layers of dirt, up to 200 feet thick, are enough to protect groundwater (and the Columbia River) from highly dangerous radioactive wastes stored in leaking tanks, ditches and holding ponds. Now it is confirmed that uranium and other radioactive contaminants are moving into the groundwater and closer to the river than the Department of Energy ever imagined or acknowledged. It will take billions of dollars to control the mess and block its movement, with no guarantee of success.

Scientists, critics, and whistleblowers within the nation's largest nuclear waste facility have urged preventative and remedial action at Hanford for years, only to be met with accusations of disloyalty and lack of expertise. As the Seattle Times recently editorialized, it is less important to determine "whether DOE (Department of Energy) was a pack of liars or just plain stupid," but urgent that Congress agrees to pay to get the contaminants under control. The radiation threat is assessed to last 20,000 years.

Reformulation award: MTBE is a highly volatile, poisonous chemical additive to gasoline which helps generate oxygen and thus makes automobile engines burn cleaner. In order to comply with federal and state Clean Air Act standards, the oil industry opted to sell mainly MTBE-methanol reformulated gasoline in California beginning in 1996. But nobody bothered to figure out that gas station tank leaks can contaminate groundwater, thus ruining drinking supplies. Some cities have already lost half their local groundwater because of MTBE. Nobody knows quite what to do. Red flags of warning are flying as an old parody song hit revives: "Don't drink the water, don't breathe the air."

Ostrich award (head-in-sand department): Those who ridicule the threat of global climate change and warming from carbon emissions, deserve a raspberry of recognition. As propagandized by talk-show whiz-bang Rush Limbaugh, the threat of global climate change is a baseless theory concocted by environmental "whackos" and harebrained radicals trying to monkey-wrench big business.

Conveniently overlooked are certain facts set forth in 1995 in a careful appraisal affirmed by 2,500 of the world's top climate scientists: the 10 hottest years on record all occurred since 1980; an unusual increase in catastrophic super-storms; recent, rapid melting of European and tropical mountain glaciers; disintegration of Antarctic ice shelves; warming of Alaskan soils; rising ocean surface temperatures, etc. (post 2000 statistics underscore the seriousness of the trends).

All the while, the fossil industries, generating untoward amounts of CO_2 into the atmosphere, have spent millions subsidizing a handful of scientists who deride any connection between gaseous industry and climate destabilization. Their public relations arms work the Washington political scene, better to cloud the public mind. So much for objectivity and "talk-show science."

Reverberation award: A huge (1997) study by the National Cancer Institute indicates that perhaps 50,000 Americans may have developed thyroid cancer from radioactive fallout. The source: nuclear bomb tests in the Nevada desert in the 1950's. This is not meant to relate to nuclear power plants, except as a possible worst case scenario. The victims resided in a belt of states stretching from Nevada to the East Coast, all subject to vagaries of the westerly winds and the secrecy and culpability of the former Atomic Energy Commission, which steadfastly lied about the situation. The new study underscores the heroism of Nobel winner Linus Pauling, who led the way, compiling petitions with factual criticism of nuclear test policy by thousands of scientists. Finally the U.S. and USSR signed the 1961 atmospheric test ban.

"Those who forget the mistakes of the past are doomed to repeat them."

Postscript: Writing some twelve years after 1997, new concerns have arisen about the safety of current moves to re-license old, and in some cases decrepit nuclear power plants, especially those that do not meet current safety guidelines. Yet, the Nuclear Regulatory Commission has gone ahead, granting 20 year license renewals for continued operation to almost half the existing plants, allowing some to increase their power output beyond their original maximum. Bedeviled with corrosion and rust, embrittled metal and hidden welds almost impossible to survey, no one can say with certainty that risks have been eliminated; rather, more likely, they have been greatly magnified by the move to keep these old plants producing power, while projected new plants struggle to get approved and eventually go on line. The Diablo Canyon plant in San Luis Obispo County is among those filing for a twenty year renewal license, even as recent geological studies report the finding of another earthquake fault only one mile away. Anyone who thinks the nuclear power debate is over and that the major issues have been resolved is only fooling himself. And the assertion that the nuclear path is "carbon free" neglects to account for the millions of tons of carbon emissions that are a direct product of ten or more years of construction of every new nuclear power station.

A GLOWING WARNING FROM RITA AND KATRINA

Anyone who watched the mad scenes of tens of thousands of people trying to flee Galveston, Houston and New Orleans in the face of these hurricanes cannot help but be skeptical of plans for hurried emergency evacuation of SLO county in the face of a nuclear-plant accident.

At least those fleeing in Texas and Louisiana had ample warning of the storm and a variety of freeways and air routes to get out of town. Better yet, they had no fear of invisible deadly radiation and had plenty of time to get their families together and make a decision. Still, even given these advantages, the exodus was snarled by traffic congestion and was at times chaotic.

Just imagine the same kind of scenario caused by emergency mandatory calls to leave our town and area. Most people would think first of their children and how to get them. The roads would be quickly filled with cars and the kind of gridlock we saw in the South. Since radiation is undetectable without scientific equipment, people would continuously wonder just what direction they should steer and whether wind changes would render their choices random and invalid. Radio and telephone lines would be jammed with callers. Fleeing in panic, last-minute deciders would further bottle up the roads and add to the confusion.

Despite all the planned siren warnings and broadcast instructions of escape routes, isn't it about time that we acknowledge that we are living with an illusion of safety? At least the people of Texas and Louisiana and Mississippi will be mostly able to return home after the storms pass. Not so for us residents of the Central Coast if a release of radiation, however deemed unlikely, makes the crops and ground radioactive.

Some people, perhaps many people, will say that kind of scenario for Diablo Canyon and San Luis Obispo and Santa Barbara County is highly problematic and unlikely to occur. That's what was said about the likelihood of a hurricane swamping New Orleans head on. And so it was said about the "unsinkable" Titanic.

-Not Published

A MOVIE OASIS: PALM THEATRE WITH SOLAR ARRAY ON ROOF.

WHY CAN'T WE ACCEPT THE SCIENCE OF GLOBAL WARMING?

The ice storms that paralyzed parts of northern New York and New England and much of Canada raise warning flags of climate destabilization. It also brought back some memories.

Fresh out of college, I spent a beautiful summer running a golf driving range on the flanks of Mt. Washington, N.H. One splendid August day, I made the summit by bush-whacking up the steep slopes after somehow losing the trail. In retrospect, it wasn't smart, as that mountain's unpredictable weather is famous for changing from balmy to subfreezing in an hour or less.

At 6,288 feet, Mt. Washington is the highest peak in the northeast United States. In 1934, mountain wind velocity was clocked at 231 mph- the highest ever recorded on Earth (until the typhoon that hit Guam in 1997).

In a television interview during the ice storms, the governor of Maine pointed to a startling fact: For the first time in the history of Mt. Washington, temperatures were actually higher on the summit than they were at the base. But how could that be? Temperature drops 3.3 degrees Fahrenheit for every 1,000 feet of elevation gain. At that rate, the temperature of top of Mt. Washington should have been 15-plus degrees colder than at the bottom, and likely colder than that because of the wind.

The reason for the strange inversion signals a warning: moist, tropical air, part of the El Nino pattern affecting the jet stream, was blown far off its usual course at the same time that frigid arctic air flowed into the region. The cold, heavier air underlay the rising warm airflow, forcing a tropical precipitation to fall through freezing layers. Imagine! -- tropical air in New Hampshire in January!

In his fascinating book, "The End of Nature," Bill McKibben explains the vast consensus among climate scientists who find that the earth's atmosphere is indeed heating, mainly as a function of the escalating burning of fossil fuels and the resultant production of carbon dioxide. As the planet's atmosphere heats, temperatures rise over vast expanses of surface ocean water, generating ever more intense storms and unpredictable, strange variations from usual weather patterns.

Of course, as McKibben notes, the illusion of a big scientific controversy over the threat of climate change is a sham, fostered by the fossil fuel industry and a handful of industry-funded scientists. As was the case with tobacco interests denying for a generation any link between smoking and lung cancer, a huge fuel industry effort aims at creating doubt about the scientific indications; the mass media is lured to report a need for years of further research to "prove" a linkage between emissions and climate destabilization.

Human burning activities, whether of forests or by automobile and industrial emissions, are precipitously adding to the atmospheric burden. Carbon pools from deep within the Earth, which in the case of coal and oil represent hundreds of millions of years of storage, are being released to the atmosphere in the blindingly brief geologic span of fewer than 200 years.

In effect, the natural order and cleaning-time processes of nature are being choked off and defeated. Along with genetic cloning, this marks the end of nature's control of the planet- what McKibben calls "the end of nature" as it has functioned from the beginning of time.

The year 1997 was the warmest year in recorded weather history. The 10 warmest global years on record all occurred since 1980. Polls show, McKibben notes, that most Americans believe in the green-house effect, but they won't pay a nickel gas tax to help offset it." We would rather live in fantasy and pretend our ills will magically go away. It is much like watching in giddy time-warp the young heroine in the block-buster film, "Titanic." Not satisfied with the real-life drama of Titanic's actual passengers, Hollywood created a fictional love story. The heroine sloshes through the bowels of the sinking liner to free her lover chained in the brig. Carefully forgotten are the effects of being continually sprayed and soaked with frigid ocean water as she pulls off the rescue and is eventually plucked from the North Atlantic whole and happy. And the viewing public laps it up.

Are our brains iced from too much fantasy? Why can't we accept truth as stranger than fiction? It is!

Can we awaken people to act toward preventing further climate destabilization? Formal education is too theoretical, too glacial. We need something immediate and practical, perhaps a device that will push us to press government and industry to move to zero-emission vehicles, and industry to pay true environmental costs.

Motor vehicles could be equipped to display dollar operating costs per mile (e.g.: SLO to Santa Maria @ $0.65 per mile comes to around $20. And a "carbon-meter" would show total carbon dioxide ejected into the air (the actual rate is five pounds for every gallon of gasoline consumed.) The gauges would be a constant reminder to driver and passengers to economize.

Airline environmental costs also need scrutiny, because airplanes, especially taking-off, contribute a huge burden of CO_2 to the earth's atmosphere. Government, industry, and the public must awaken. Otherwise, our children will face the inevitable consequences in the form of ruined harvests, scorching droughts or super-storms and floods, astronomical insurance rates, and, perhaps, forced migration from flooded coastal areas. Such is the direction of a mindless escapism, our continuing failure to deal with the full scope of the problem, our obsessive search for fantasy...while the band plays on.

LOS ANGELES FREEWAY TO HEAVEN!
- THE ABSURDITY OF IT ALL

LAST EXIT ON THE "FREE-WAY" – ENERGY CRISIS AND LIFESTYLE

The least recognized aspect of $5-a-gallon gasoline is that it marks the end of the line for continuing urban sprawl. No more will it be credible or profitable to play for speculative riches by holding farmland and open space distant from the city core.

The daily commute will become far too expensive to support the suburban living habit, which has long been the bane of balanced city planning. Driving from Paso Robles or Santa Maria to San Luis Obispo, for example, at 60 cents a mile or more in actual automobile support costs (including insurance, maintenance, wear on the car and fuel) is a powerful disincentive for shopping trips and all but the most necessary jaunts. Even the most car-addicted will begin to reckon the necessity of each trip when out of pocket costs create empty wallets and severely burden credit card balances.

The dream of a single family home way out in the country has become affordable only to the super rich. For commuters who are trapped in a lifestyle of long hours on the road, the situation is much worse. They don't have the option of simply not going to work, although telecommuting will become more and more of a pattern for many businesses.

Why have we Americans gone on so long believing that the world will never change to undermine our extravagant and wasteful ways of life? We have had more warnings than even many so-called experts recognize. Here are a few:

- In 1952, President Truman's Materials Policy Commission warned in "Resources for Freedom" about dependence on oil from the Middle East. Weighing the relative merits of solar versus nuclear power development, the special panel on energy policy concluded that nuclear power is not the way to energy freedom and urged instead "aggressive research in the whole field of solar energy"

  Truman left office and Gen. Eisenhower became president. He, too, had to review energy options but had the bad fortune to be advised by high energy physicists who had a guilt complex

117

over the use of the atomic bomb, and by huge corporations that had strong monetary interests in the development of "atoms for peace." The program was sold to the president and the country in an intense wave of advertising that promised an energy future in which the atom would produce energy too cheap to meter. Today, this PR campaign can be seen as laughable, but back then a gullible public was rather quickly convinced of the plan. The cost of that mistake easily adds up into the trillions of dollars in lost productive investment and gross over-dependence on foreign oil and nuclear power at energy prices that break all American records.

European and other industrialized nations pay far more for gasoline both then and now- some exceeding $7 a gallon. And nuclear power or coal (most electricity in the United States is produced by burning coal) can't provide the 25 percent of national energy required by cars and trucks, plus the approximately 18 percent needed for space and water heating.

One of the first energy policies of both Bush administrations was to cut the solar energy research and development budget in half. Fossil fuel and nuclear power interests and advocates have maintained or are beginning again increased dominance in policy making.

- In 1974, the Ford Foundation's Energy Policy Project stressed the need for a shift in transportation away from commuting and toward the redesign of cities for much greater energy conservation.

- Again in 1974, President Nixon's Technical Review on Energy Independence recommended a much larger budget for solar research and development, but the report was smoke-screened by the then Atomic Energy Commission, which proposed a budget of only 5 percent of that given to nuclear research.

And so it has gone until the current crisis, because of stall and drift and the dominance of heavy energy investment in fossil fuels and nuclear power, with their enormous and subsidized capital costs. Today, because of spiking fuel costs and the huge problem of greenhouse gases and carbon dioxide emissions, we hear the cry again for huge investments in expanding nuclear power.

Little is said in the constant promotional ads on TV about the enormous costs of construction ($10 billion to $15 billion estimated for each nuclear plant). Nor do we hear in advertisements about the safety problems associated with nuclear waste storage, the 10- to 13-year time lapse before a plant becomes operational and the consequent loss (again) of investment dollars for solar, wind, geothermal and other "soft" energy alternatives that can be brought on line more quickly and cheaply.

As the British journal The Ecologist noted in a study concluded in 2008, the course of construction of a nuclear power station creates some 20 million tons of carbon dioxide added to the atmosphere. And all this says nothing about the enormous untapped possibilities of energy conservation, which still stands as our greatest resource.

In 1973, the Rand Corporation estimated that California would have to build a 1,000 megawatt nuclear plant for every two miles of coastline just to keep up with then projected demand. That report to the Legislature pretty much scotched the whole idea of reliance on nuclear. Simpler solutions are much better ways to work out of the energy crunch. Better regional planning, green-building and mandating hybrid and other conservation technologies for all government-purchased vehicles are three solid examples of wise action.

Falling back on highly expensive and wasteful options eats up not just billions of dollars, but time itself- the greatest unmeasured resource of each generation.

*   *   *   *   *

Postscript: Beginning in 2008 , the proposal to build an industrial-size solar power installation out on the Carrizo (Carrisa) Plains, north and east of San Luis Obispo, has split the environmental community. It is not just the immense size of the proposed installation, but the fact that it would be built on sensitive habitat and affect endangered species that has pushed old friends and green allies into warring camps. If built as planned, it would be the largest solar-electric producing plant in the United States; the plan has the backing of many conservation stalwarts as well as large solar companies. But many conservationists are also strongly opposed.

Basically, the argument boils down to centralized power installation with huge capacity to produce electric power from a unique single source as opposed to decentralized planning for local electricity production such as rooftop collectors. The latter would eliminate the loss of power that inheres in transmission lines, and would insure that the Carrisa Plains environment would remain essentially rural and permanently protected for wild and endangered species and as a place for human visitation to relatively primitive land.

As I see it, there is room for a great compromise between the two viewpoints.

Rooftop solar collection should be a mandate for every community in the county and incentives should quickly be put in place to achieve that end, including buy-back by utilities of electric power so produced. A county-wide audit of rooftop collection sites and possibilities should be the first step. The results could then be tied to a solar plant, built in stages, and of much smaller size and less footprint at Carrisa. As these projects continue building in tandem, with a percentage of money from solar plant generation being re-circulated to the rooftop plan, it should be much more possible to mitigate and perhaps eliminate any egregious effects. A final decision on size should be held in abeyance until more is known about the possibilities of a dual plan.

RE-IMAGINING CITIES

"Urban Design After the Age of Oil"
Liveblog conference: Nov. 6-8, 2008

The Future of Automobility: posted online by Lloyd Alter, architect, (on-line response: Ira Winn and others...)

"Moderator Charles Waldheim wonders about the future of automobility, and how well we will design out cities after the car is gone. I must confess that I thought this was the single biggest question of this conference, the issue that defines the nature of urban development in our culture.

Surprisingly, the question has rarely come up so far in the sessions that I have attended. Perhaps it is because not many of the architects at this conference actually believe that we are going to have to live without automobility.

One contributor suggests that we are not going to get rid of cars; they may be different but without them we will not be able to get to any of the places that we built that depend on them.

Another suggests that we think about cars because they are destroying our atmosphere, but adds that we should think more about how cars are destroying our cities. He actually thinks that it is crazy that people hold up the Prius as an example of how technology will save us, when in fact the Smart Car gets better mileage with less input, less technology. It is just smaller. We don't necessarily need fancy new technologies, just better and smarter distribution of resources. But he still thinks we are going to have cars. Another participant here looks forward to the day that we have all those little cars as storage units that can become part of the national energy grid; we don't have to get rid of cars, we just have to make them part of the system.

Moderator: I am a bit shocked. I would have thought that the single biggest factor affecting urban design in the age after oil is the virtual elimination of private cars, replaced by denser, walkable cities, transit and bicycles. I am a bit surprised. Are you?

Comments:

From: Pasadena, CA

Oil ! = Cars. Ultralight plug-in biofuel-hybrid, or battery-electric, or fuel cell powered vehicles can, and will step into the void left by today's cars after oil becomes permanently, impractically expensive. If we want dense, walkable, bikeable, livable cities, we can't count on the end of the Oil Age to get us there. It only looks that way now, because we haven't put much effort into transitioning our fleet vehicles away from oil. People cut back on driving to save money, because they don't have many other choices. We can seize this opportunity to get transit and livable street measures enacted, while people are open to change, but if we fail to do so, automotive technology will change, and we'll be left with the same sprawling mess we've got now, only it will be immune to future large commodity price swings, making it all the harder to get rid of.

from San Luis Obispo, CA : Winn suggests that if the U.S. government would notify automakers that starting next year it will buy ONLY fleet or individual government vehicles that get at least 45 miles per gallon, it would go a long way to providing the necessary manufacturing incentive for change. The government buys hundreds of thousands of vehicles each year.

Also, while there is legitimate focus on commuting, a deeper problem is getting people out of their vehicles and slowing the habit of driving as a psychological escape from boredom and feeling locked in. Livable, walkable cities will do much to break the auto "habit". We can't do that without good transit options, such as the experiments in Boston and a few other cities on computerized car-sharing (e.g.:Zipcard) which does much to negate dependency on a personal automobile. Also, once there are valid options for movement, it will be much easier for people to negate fears of travel in smaller vehicles exposed to streets filled with monstrous sized cars. The object of movement will become the delight of going and seeing rather than "getting there" in a fool's rush.

A contributor in Washington, DC writes:

This is not rocket science folks. I envision a series of bullet trains traveling north and south, east and west. They will travel non-stop between major cities or transfer points (every 100 miles). These trains would intersect at these major cities and transfer points to less congested smaller cities and rural towns, with metro-like trains, to take travelers to other mass-transit sources (buses). The car as a source of long distance travel would be impractical or obsolete. Cars would be smaller and fuel efficient and only used for social networking with trips less than 50 miles.

FLASHY IDOL OF THE GOD, "RAH,"
WORSHIPPED BY MILLIONS.

A GRAVEYARD OF AUTOMOBILES AND IDOLS

VI. FESTIVAL MARKETPLACES VS. SHOPPING MALLS

CAMOUFLAGING THE RANCH

The battle over development of the Dalidio Ranch (Measure J) is hardly an argument over soccer fields, new "low cost" housing or a butterfly farm. Nor is it a question of whether Mr. Dalidio is a fine fellow, something that even most opponents of the measure acknowledge. It is, however, a debate over worrisome costs and the impacts his proposal would have on his fellow citizens and taxpayers. And it is a controversy over big Texas and Los Angeles money coming in to San Luis to dictate where and how the city and county will develop and grow. Is a project of such size and intensity healthy for our area?

The Dalidio Ranch, formerly the Marketplace, had taken a different form than that which was submitted to and rejected by San Luis city voters. As its proponents declared when introducing it to the press and the public- this is an entirely new project. Whether it really is "entirely new" is debatable.

New projects or projects changed in significant ways require a new environmental impact statement so the possibilities and strategies for correcting or mitigating adverse effects can be publicly revealed and discussed. This is not a matter of nuisance or quirky procedure. Plain and simple, it's the law, and it aims at protecting the public and the environment. It applies to projects large and small, when first presented for consideration by government or when changed in major ways. Project proponents may claim that the environmental ground has already been tilled, but an environmental report was never certified for this project.

But hold everything! In this situation, involving a ballot initiative petition, the Dalidio project is not bound by the usual rules. If passed by the voters of San Luis Obispo County, the project is automatically exempted from the usual protective city procedures, with startling implications for all communities in the county. Not only will it duck meeting an environmental review process, it will set the stage by precedent for bypassing local control. Any community in this county can then have projects stuffed down their throats by big money developers wishing to avoid the test of local community oversight. A countywide ballot can override local opinion, be it the placement of a sewer plant, the coming of a Wal-Mart or other controversial efforts. Further, the affected city or cities will have very little managerial control and input, even though infrastructure effects and costs may be heavy.

What all this means is that approval of the Dalidio Ranch projects is bound to bring a slew of lawsuits over implementation issues of sewer, water, roads, access, grading, costs, etc. At stake will be millions of dollars in taxpayer money to be paid out in suits that will make lawyers richer and residents apoplectic. If you like the Los Osos sewer marathon, you'll just love the Dalidio Ranch sweepstakes.

The city of San Luis Obispo will bear the brunt of environmental impacts and huge associated costs. The City Council is well aware of this and would much prefer that the project comes back to city jurisdiction, even though city voters denied the project in last year's election. Without a reasonable compromise between city, county, developer and the environmental community and citizenry in general, the Ranch project is a deadening threat to all that is progressive and wise in urban planning and development. As it stands, the Dalidio Ranch's 500,000 square feet of commercial space dwarfs the entire retail footage of downtown San Luis Obispo and presents a serious challenge to the continuing economic viability of the city core.

Changes in the Ranch proposal, compared with the earlier version known as the Marketplace, underscore the need for full and rigorous environmental review. The Prado Road overpass has been deleted, leaving the puzzling question of where all the new traffic will be dumped without creating nightmare blockage on already impacted area roads and on Highway 101. A new wastewater treatment plant is planned to sit over the aquifer near Los Osos Valley Road and the freeway, and the projected soccer fields nearby. Will the water quality control boards be able to exert jurisdiction and control over these critical aspects of health and sanitation? Or does the Ranch get a "free pass" by ballot? And why soccer fields in an area that might better be used for mud wrestling? The aquifer involved on Dalidio land is the last potential water supply for the city and might better be taken by eminent domain for the benefit of all. Certainly, this benefit is worthy of debate.

Many other issues, old and new, remain on the table- the loss of prime agricultural land chief among them. The Dalidio Ranch initiative is a faulty way to face these problems by end-running environmental laws. Let's hope the public is not confused by the expedient of a countywide ballot. On election day we need to remember that voting for the Ranch proposal will only set the stage for endless and fruitless acrimony. We need to look well before we leap.

Letters Editor:

COUNTY WILL VACUUM REVENUE

The letter writer who responded to my article on the Dalidio Ranch project has a weird sense of himself and of Measure J. He "disqualifies" me, an urban studies professor, from commenting on the dangers of unbalanced growth in the town in which I live. Why? Because I failed to correctly identify the composer of a 1940's theme song made popular by Gen Miller and his orchestra. Wow.

Over a 35-year career, I have consulted on environmental issues to several countries and public agencies, and have taught a number of courses on urban problems. I have evaluated Measure J, and I ask only that people draw their own conclusions based on reason.

I do have one last question for people who think only San Luis Obispo city will be hit with paying for the Ranch proposal. This enormous retail development will vacuum sales tax income from every store and every city in the county, which will pour into the county treasury. How will the county reimburse towns from Paso Robles to Nipomo and beyond for their lost tax dollars? And how will the county and city pay for the infrastructure costs still unknown when they can't even keep the library open full time to serve the public?

SQUEAKING WHEELS

Some big downtown wheels are beginning to squeak, as the realization dawns that building shopping malls on the city's periphery will have negative consequences for our traditional commercial center.

Mr. Copeland and other downtown promoters and merchants are upset that the Dalidio/Marketplace project off Los Osos Valley Road will attract "lifestyle businesses" that will compete with retail downtown, including his Downtown Centre and proposed retail-office projects on Court, Palm, and Monterey streets. The downtowners had hoped to have their cake and eat it too, and, in the benefit of hindsight, are likely wishing they had opposed mall development on the southern edge of San Luis Obispo right from the beginning. The Chamber of Commerce and the Downtown Business Association also had (have?) their heads in the sand.

For as Mr. King, the owner of the Fremont Theater, put it so well in a recent Opinion piece in the Tribune, once a project is approved there is no telling how competitive or even who the new lessees are going to be; he concludes that the development on Dalidio will hurt, maybe kill, our beloved downtown.

One would have thought that any leader would be aware of what has already happened to hundreds of downtowns as a result of edge-development of urban malls. But money talks big to our mayor and City Council, hypnotized as they are by the prospect of sales tax revenues that they can then spend on still another concrete pour that can't pay for itself. As some wag remarked, "Why not be honest with us and rename Los Osos Valley Road from Madonna to the 101 freeway? Call it "Sales Tax Receipts Avenue".

One might argue that the same fears for downtown were expressed when the original Madonna Mall was proposed. But that mall was poorly planned and stillborn and cannot be compared to what is now building there and in the surrounding area: Best Buy Electronics, Home Depot, Macy's, Target, a fancy new hotel, Borders Books, Petco, Costco, and who knows what else? Can the relatively slow growing county population support all this development? More likely, we are starting a war of attrition in which the slices of pie grow progressively smaller and local merchants are forced out by the chain stores, which send their profits largely out of the county instead of re-circulating them within. And the new downtown projects are also largely high rent, blocking out small local enterprises.

These are questions rarely asked by the City Council, even as they shy away from asking about cumulative impacts of all these developments, demands for services, costs of future maintenance, and diversion of investments from areas of dire need.

Look at the so-called compromise plan for Dalidio . The original offer of the developer included 28 acres of senior and working class housing, twin soccer fields, and a senior center, all of which were bargained away for more stores as well as some open space. The rationale is that the area is in the airport flight path and is thereby "dangerous." Is an airplane crashing into a crowded Macy's, for example, less dangerous than one crashing into a recreation soccer field? It doesn't take the Defense Department to figure that one out.

Let's not forget, this is prime agricultural land that will be covered in concrete. This project is a launch pad for a bridge widening and overpass, so to connect with still more development in the airport area. It's justified in the name of sales tax revenue and as a way of hopefully (from the city view) forestalling the county from taking on other projects --which they can still do on nearby land. One project is used to breed another, that also cannot pay for itself.

Meanwhile, the very real needs of low-cost housing, education, watershed protection, and dealing with the health care crisis are pushed onto the back burners. They don't generate sales tax revenue, only a better quality of life for the city and county. It's "planning" by segregated projects with little thought to cumulative costs and effects on the downtown.

"I told 'em, you told 'em, we all told 'em. But they never seem to wake up."

THE MARKETPLACE: A TROJAN HORSE

Hidden behind all the rhetoric advocating the shopping mall known as The Marketplace (aka the Ranch) is a breach in the wall of protection that keeps San Luis Obispo almost unique among smaller towns.

Mall proponents do not add in the negative financial consequences to the city. It is more than simply excusing the fact of the proposed kickback of tax revenues by the city to the developer. It is more than the admission that the proposed housing element is a fig leaf obscuring the fact that the vast majority of new employees will, because of real estate prices, have to find places to live far outside San Luis Obispo; this will increase the commuter traffic problem as well as burden surrounding towns with issues that we do not wish to face squarely here at home. It is more than the fact that the county as well as the state are in fiscal crisis, making it highly unlikely that the financial ability exists to move the development into the county, even if the county should so wish- an aspect totally avoided in the scare tactics literature by mall proponents. It is more than the clogging of local roads.

And it is more than the fact that the many chain stores being implanted with the new developments send the majority of their sales dollars out of the county and even out of the state. All of these issues point to a breach in local monetary circulation and a make-over of San Luis Obispo to a copycat image of so many defunct and dreary towns.

But the Trojan Horse that is The Marketplace goes beyond these aspects. And even beyond the high, recurring costs of interest-bearing bond issues for infrastructure- sewers, roads, police and fire, education impacts etc. A "Yes" on ballot measures A, B, and C sends a signal to developers around the country that San Luis has become an open ground for future large scale development. After all, the money and push for The Marketplace comes mainly from Texas and L.A. developers. And even if that were not so, a real hidden issue remains that ties the marketplace to the famous horse of Troy.

Here I point to the oft-obscured fact that development breeds ever more development, that The Marketplace is not the end of the road. Proposals are already in the planning that are dependent on the building of the Dalidio-Bird (Marketplace) project. For one the Prado Road overpass is essential to the build-out of the Airport annexation area. Other projects are lined up like bulldozers awaiting future action by the city council. The ABC ballot is an invitation for more of the same (vote "yes") or a signal flag that it is time to re-think the whole process and change direction (vote "no").

So instead of having the full advantages to the city of sales tax revenues from this or any given project, a huge portion of any such revenues will be given away or otherwise earmarked for still more store development down the road. More development means more bond issues and still more debt for the city. Each debt builds on the next in a giant pyramid scheme that can only result in some future fiscal catastrophe. This is the real Trojan horse! It subverts key issues such as housing, health, library services, open space, education, a viable and esthetic downtown, and the quality of life here in our city. A "No" on ABC is a vote for the future heath of San Luis Obispo.

However, the voters in the county voted "Yes".

Note: The Marketplace project has long been in limbo as a result of a lower court ruling invalidating a Board of Supervisors decision that provided for a county-wide election to overturn a city vote against the project. In August 2009, the Appellate Court reversed the earlier decision declaring that the county voters do have the right to put in play their initiative and overturn the voters of the city. In October 2009, the California Supreme Court rejected an appeal by the plaintiffs, leaving standing the Appeals court decision. This last ruling leaves a huge quandary for the developer, who has to decide whether and how to proceed with his project in the face of a down-turned economy and environmental requirements. As well, it leaves the puzzle of how any city can protect itself against moves by highly financed outside interests, who threaten to enlarge the voting base beyond city boundaries whenever they fear a city vote will go against their partisan position. The decision not to review the case is bound to lead to much future legal wrangling.

VAST EXPANSE OF PARKING FOR BOX STORES ON LOS OSOS
VALLEY ROAD;

PRIZE WINNING COURT STREET CENTER

A CURMUDGEONLY VIEW OF TWO ARCHITECTURES

Thousands of visitors a week come to the billion-dollar Getty Museum in Los Angeles. I'm unsure of how they interpret what they see, but here I react to two contrasting kinds of architecture in two different environments. This is what they tell me.

A few months after it opened to the public, I visited the sprawling museum complex that dominates the posh Bel Air and Brentwood suburbs- to the consternation of many residents. Who would have dreamed that millions of eyes would one day peer down at once-private and secluded back yards? Or that the view up the chaparral slopes would end at a gigantic construction?

Following a sound basic dictum of architect Frank Lloyd Wright, a building should never be set on top of a hill. Construction should be set into the hill to save the natural beauty and have the best of both worlds- the house and the hilltop. Human ego often says otherwise. Viewed from the Bel Air hills, the Getty under construction appeared as a massive gash in the Santa Monica mountains, a jumble of buildings set atop an entire ridge line. It speaks of the medieval fortress mentality. In time, of course, it will be somewhat shielded by trees. Difficult to access on foot (it's forbidden), it hovers aloof from the larger community it has pledged to serve.

Within the Getty there are marvelous touches and fantastic views over the sprawling city and, on clear days, out to the Pacific ocean. There are beautifully lighted galleries, much open space, some interesting fountains and plantings, and a feeling of touching the sky. These are its intrinsic strengths.

The Getty has become a major tourist attraction, complete with monorail and bus ride and elaborate parking scenarios. Like Grauman's Chinese Theatre in Hollywood or the Disney Concert Hall it's one of the "must see" edifices to visit in L.A. But for all the years of planning and zillions of dollars expended, it should be far better:

- The hilltop location is a wind-draw. During less-than-perfect weather; the open eating areas become uncomfortable, and assaulted by flying paper plates and napkins. Many of the non-native plants simply can't survive that exposed and often foggy location. Hidden under the brow of the hill, the museum would be better protected and not be an overbearing presence for the community below.

- Maintenance costs are extravagant ($100,000 to wash the windows). The Italian stone façade was cut in an unusual way to better reflect light, but the downside is an already worrisome deterioration. Water bills are excessive. The inordinate burden of upkeep has forced severe cuts in the once priority education program.

- Exterior walls are half-surfaced with a wonderfully soft, glimmering travertine. The other half has a façade of large metal plates or squares cut to the same size as the stone. The white squares, especially, clash with the travertine and accentuate the feeling of unmatched buildings in both shape and color. Further, the un-mortared stone gives the appearance of being glued to the concrete walls behind, diminishing, rather than enhancing, what should be a feeling of strength and support. Those open cracks, I noticed, draw youngsters with irresistible alpinist dreams.

- The geometry of the central garden is striking when viewed from above, but it left me cold when deep in its heart. The artificial stream that winds to the garden is "hokey," with large angular rocks that could only have been placed by a fashion designer. The zigzag walkway with its metal retaining walls forces a crazy march down to the central circle; the visitor is bounced from manicured, putting green banks to bunched wild grass areas to closely spaced, pole-straight sycamores planted stream-side, almost forbidden to follow their natural bent to grow crooked.

The central garden ends in dull gravel banks blocking the view of the cityscape below, so the visitor will supposedly focus on either the azalea circle, when in bloom, or the almost random flower assortments. It's rationalized as an artistic-design tribute to multifaceted L.A.- but it's too forced and unconnected. Just as well place automobile parts amidst the blooms and call it L.A.'s contribution to California technology and culture.

So much for my impressions of site and architecture. Art experts can write of the important art within the walls. Suffice to say, money does not guarantee artistic greatness, as we in San Luis must learn from architectural perversions in the form of super-stores and shopping malls. Our newest additions on Broad Street-Marigold and on Los Osos Valley Road smack of San Quentin style -- stockades of concrete block stores surrounding huge exercise yards for cars. Trying to cross on foot is to put one's life at risk.

Here, anyone seeking organic design, an integrated view of the hills, a dynamic marketplace of human scale is headed for a serious case of the blahs. It's all geared to ringing the cash register, with nary a nod to the many virtues and profits of window shopping and pausing to exchange pleasantries in a public agora. Instead, the design tells us, "Hurry up and buy something, and then go home." It's another example of loose screening by an architectural review panel that apparently would be hard-pressed to find much difference between a hippopotamus and a petunia.

We have to open our eyes and become seekers and seers, or we'll end up robotized consumers of whatever big money throws at us. Or haven't you noticed?

A GREENER MARKETPLACE

Letters to the Editors
SLO County TRIBUNE

Congratulations to the architecture students producing models for a greener Marketplace.

They have pinned down the design problems accurately: the need for major pedestrian orientation, so terribly lacking in the Bird and later models; the lack of integration of sufficient housing in the overall design; the failure to emphasize alternative energy resources; and, perhaps most critical from a design standpoint, the focus on an outmoded and anti-pedestrian central automobile parking court ruins any effort to put a human face on the project.

Last fall, Mr. Bird (the original developer) wrote to me and complained about my pointing out deficiencies in the Marketplace design, as well as the location- where it is sure to increase traffic jams in an important corridor as well as drawing business out of the downtown. In responding to his letter, I pointed out that the circulation element of the SLO General Plan gives priority to avoiding dominance of the automobile, to say nothing of the basic principle of saving prime farmland. "It's never to late to learn," I noted.

The architecture students are way ahead of the shopping center developers when it comes to thinking of major development in terms of building for sustainability and for maximizing the potential for human interaction and window shopping.

THE FESTIVAL MARKETPLACE IS SUPERIOR

The festival market is a place of exchange for both merchandise and ideas. It is where people can break out of the isolation of city living. Webster's Collegiate Dictionary defines a mall as " a public area, often set with shade trees and designed as a promenade or as a pedestrian walk." The definition has become antiquated by poor practice.

People linger in a true marketplace because of the variety of activities. By contrast, the mall as we know it today has become sterile because it is heavily focused on shopping, and the central area is taken up with automobiles. Our Downtown Centre, for example, is an exciting place to spend time and money. By contrast, the malls on Tank Farm Road and on most of Los Osos ValleyRoad are not joyful places to linger and exchange ideas. The message of the architecture is "please spend your money and go home." Simply crossing the central "court of parking" is hazardous to pedestrians. With design foresight, the whole experience could have been enriched by placement of parking areas off to the side. The smart and dynamic mall keeps pedestrianism as a top priority.

James Rouse, the acclaimed planner-developer of the festival marketplace concept, favored small stores, even pushcart enterprises, over chain stores. He stressed variety of food and merchandise and the ambiance of a festival-- moving water, balloons, benches, performances. Whether shopping, eating, discussing or watching, the *buzz* is infectious; it draws large crowds and the cash-registers ring merrily. What rubbing elbows produces in ideas, new directions, and an escape from urban loneliness can never be measured, but it is there. Quite a contrast to our frumpy malls!

When the Downtown Association put the squeeze on the SLO Marketplace, it forced the developer to turn his original plan for a kind of festival market into just another mall. The downtown lobby was afraid that a real marketplace would provide solid competition- an alternate fine place to shop and hang-out. They convinced the Council to restrict competition and limit success.

There are better reasons for opposing the SLO Marketplace or Ranch: its potential for contributing to huge traffic snarls on and near Los Osos Valley Road; and its horrific cementing of prime farmland. As a critic of urban trends I have long argued against box store expansion on the urban edge. I am aware of the perils posed by our City Council's fixation on sales tax revenue development. When I ask if the multitude of projected new stores will adversely affect local merchants, I am greeted with "that's the competitive way."

Why is it o.k. to limit competition with downtown, but not o.k. to do the same for established businesses such as Quaglino's and the Pacific Home Center, outside downtown? Let's face it: ALMOST ALL LOCAL BUSINESS will be adversely affected by the chains. They sell almost everything from lamps to bicycles to towels; from lumber to carpeting to pharmaceuticals; from optics to video equipment to jewelry etc. Hiring a consultant to say the opposite should fool no one.

The big developers from outside continue scouting for new mall areas in our county. They are being courted by hungry city councils. The whole strategy amounts to an expensive house of cards that promotes sameness over uniqueness. San Luis can command the county sales marketplace only so long as other cities nearby don't jump on the development bandwagon. The pie is only so big, and foolish efforts to puff up sales tax revenue are responding to a mirage—an endless array of stores filled daily with an endless parade of shoppers.

Better to invest a larger percent of our revenues on health and housing and education, and in maintaining our environmental assets. Copycat retail investment, with enormous infrastructure and service costs and dull duplication, gambles the allure and solvency of the city.

These are hard economic times. Yes, we should invest in one or two real festival marketplaces in appropriate locations. Carefully planned, these generate both locally circulating revenues and a balanced business and cultural climate... But please put an end to "mallaria"!

MARKETPLACE SOLUTION LIES 'OUTSIDE THE BOX'

Solving the riddle of Mr. Dalidio's "Marketplace" is on a line with getting the passengers to push a trolley-car that has lost its power. It's hard work, but it can be done.

San Luis Obispo is split wide on the issues of growth, and the huge Dalidio/Bird box-store Marketplace planned off Los Osos Valley Road is now the number one development paradox. Concerned retail interests are funding a re-study of the 2002 analysis, which concluded that there will be little negative effect on downtown business.

It is said that things have changed. In our county, known for sponsoring high-priced studies to back already arrived at conclusions, one wonders what is next? If the existing study is suspect after only two years, any new prognosis will also be shaky as things change again. Gosh, it's not rocket science. Anyone with horse-sense knows that mall development on city edge is hardly Gator-Aid for downtown.

Almost everyone fears the likelihood of traffic chaos at the southern boundary of the city, resulting from the 550,00- 650,000-square-foot build-out of retail space, which is more than exists in the entire downtown. And there is no way around the loss of prime farmland. Indeed, there is no workable compromise solution so long as the location of the land lies at the root of the problem. So let's try to "push the trolley."

I propose moving the entire project to a part of the city that will not have the negatives of the Dalidio farmland-development. Let's move "The Marketplace" to a position where it will not compete with the downtown, and will contribute to a pedestrian orientation. Already within the sights of SLO city planners for multi-level parking and for a multi-modal transit center are the huge lot behind the Bank of America on Santa Rosa Street and the Shell station property across from it. The fit of retail with proposed parking is clean, and prime farmland will not be turned into parking lots. That is where a large department store, a fine hotel etc. really belong- as part of our downtown, not as an outside competition to it.

Can the needed land deals and transfers of ownership occur? That question can only be answered by trying very hard. It hasn't happened yet. But the stakes are very high and the community losses are too great to allow the current situation to fester.

Certainly Mr. Dalidio should be given a percentage of development revenues to make up for about half his lost sale, and for the city's complicity in what can only be called "dumb zoning," which left the public as well as the landowner holding the bag. He remains free to sell his land to anyone interested in retaining its agricultural use.

As to the argument that it's an intrusion on private property rights, one should look to the reasons for all kinds of agricultural subsidies by the taxpaying public: lower taxes on ag land to protect our food future; subsidization of agricultural water and crops to reduce costs and provide harvest price stability. The farmer works hard under often precarious conditions and is thus a beneficiary of public support- but NOT so he can profit from closing prime farmland to farming.

As a conservative U.S. Supreme Court wisely found in the 1877 grain storage case, Munn v. Illinois: "When, therefore, one devotes his property to a use in which the public has an interest, he, in effect grants to the public an interest in that use, and must submit to be controlled by the public for the common good"... You can't fairly accept subsidy and then cry larceny when you are the one negating the basis of your grant.

Our present course is "no-win" for San Luis Obispo. To solve the challenge of the proposed Marketplace, we must think "outside the box." "It can't be done," cry the nay-sayers." "It won't be done," say the partisans. Clang, clang, says the trolley!

OLD CARNEGIE LIBRARY: HOME OF HISTORICAL SOCIETY

CRAFT EXHIBIT, SLO ART CENTER

BIG BOX DEVELOPMENT COST MORE THAN PEOPLE THINK

Judging from articles and reader comments, the three most important concerns for the future of San Luis Obispo city and county are: the growing lack of affordable housing; the exodus of local physicians and the threat of continuing decline in available hospital facilities in the face of a surging senior population; and the precarious nature of financing for maintaining quality education and environment.

Judging from the time and money spent by San Luis Obispo City Council and county supervisors, the three most important concerns for our area are attracting more and larger stores so as to yield an ever-larger sales tax revenue; bolstering the city-county image to attract more visitors; and developing areas in and around the city and county so that new, affluent populations can be housed and new commercial facilities and infrastructure developed to sustain the above two goals.

There need be no necessary contradiction between raising sales tax revenues and expending money for a better quality of life. But as the citizenry has seen, when push comes to shove, it is the non-cash flow, life issues that are pushed onto the back burners. Huge commercial developments are given all kinds of code exceptions, extensions, and rationalizations..

Every large commercial project is justified by referencing sales tax revenues. But on what are these revenues to be spent and at what cost to the taxpayer? The endless parade of big-box stores come with an assortment of expensive tangential developments, now or later, be it a Prado Road overpass, new projects in the airport area, drainage and flood control, and bridge construction and road widening in a futile effort to contain burgeoning traffic impacts created by boxy growth. And what of compounding interest costs of bond issues borne by a future generation? While the developer pays for some of this, the list of costly backup and support projects eats up any huge money benefits; fire, police and other services are expanded to meet new growth, not to better what already exists. Almost all major projects breed a "need" for still more city subsidy that could instead be directed toward quality-of-life development that is a basic need of a healthy city. Why not earmark a significant percentage of development revenue for a cutting edge new city health services to substitute for what we are losing? Why not major funding for new public transit, for teaching and library programs, for low income housing, and to bolster federal outlays for doctors so they don't flee the county? Putting all the major eggs in the big-store basket ignores the astonishing growth in online, computer shopping. In short, our local government justifies its madcap pursuit of "development" at the cost of very real human and social needs and risky box- monoculture development. All this shows signs of changing as a newly elected Board of Supervisors and Council works on changing policy in a "greener" direction.

As our mayor once explained, it is his goal to fill the flatlands with good housing and commercial development, leaving the hills for recreation. But the hills are rapidly being privatized by very expensive ranchette developments and there won't be much left over for recreation in a fully built-out populous city. Other areas have found this kind of development strategy yields a precarious result; once the flatlands begin to fill up, people flee even more to the hills. Or, as a once popular song goes, "It's Hollywood!" Drive down to Hollywood (or Santa Barbara) and take a look at the crowded hills and flatlands. There you can see the real "Back to the Future" of San Luis Obispo's myopic vision.

SHARK SIGHTINGS:

Letters Editor:

I'm a bit chewed up over your headline story on the possible reduction of beach closure time from five days to two, following a recent deadly shark attack off Avila beach.

The port San Luis Harbor District is undoubtedly being pressured by businesses that don't want the adverse publicity that follows a real shark incident or even a shark sighting. Yes, warning signs should be posted in either event, but no one seems to consider the problem from the viewpoint of the sharks.

Signs warning the public of the presence of danger should not only be put up on beaches, but should be printed in waterproof ink and placed underwater so the sharks learn to stay away from human prey for at least the two days under consideration as an ample warning time.

By the way, the ocean is not the only place in the county that sharks hang out. I've noted a number of the carnivores hanging around city halls whenever a new mall is being proposed. Sometimes you can spot them in their sharkskin suits and ties.

VII: REFLECTIONS –
A POTPOURRI

URBAN PYRAMID SCHEMES

The unraveling of the American economy because of the deflating housing bubble, deregulation of the marketplace and gross mismanagement at top levels of the banking, manufacturing, and financial empires is by now a well known story. It all amounts to a huge self-deception based on the fiction of an ever-expanding pie-- one that is half-baked in greed, myopic vision, and arrogance; together, they make fertile ground for the incredible pyramid schemes and untracked hundreds of billions of taxpayer dollars that are making front page headlines.

There are strong parallels here to what has gone on under the name of urban "development"- a rosy-eyed view of a cloudless economic future, with each new development piggy-backed financially on the ones preceding it. That too is a variety of pyramid or ponzi scheme, although less obviously so. For example, the building of a Prado Road overpass is hitched to mall developments on Los Osos Valley Road and in turn becomes the gateway to still new commercial developments in the Airport Annexation Area. The projected income from one project is used to seed future projects in a seemingly endless parade of sales tax revenue harvests. As always, there are huge attendant costs for infrastructure, bank loans and interest, inflation, upkeep, and negative pressure on the downtown economy.

Little thought has been given to the possibility of an economic downturn. Only former Council-member Mulholland has publicly raised a red flag. Nor has the quality of life been a principal point of concern. Education, public health, safety and social services do get handouts from increasing sales tax revenue, but they are among the first to be cut in a slowing economy. The vast percentage of revenues gained from these projects are simply moved along to subsidize ever more schemes in the sales tax pipeline. Almost none of the development projects of recent years have made a significant inroad in the fast growing lack of reasonably priced housing. And energy considerations, while increasingly talked about, have not been integrated to make major impact on our extravagant way of suburban living and commuting. The economic pie in SLO county is continually sliced thinner as cities and towns copy and compete with each other for the same retail trade. Development eggs are almost all in one basket.

Is the only answer to local and national problems to send people back to the shopping malls? That is simply a quick fix, better than a band-aid but hardly a long-term solution because it would return us to a world of false priorities and tunnel vision. Wise planning requires balanced growth and real diversification with a careful eye out for both calm and stormy economic periods. We end up paying a terrible price for pyramid schemes, especially as it is now known that a huge wave of mall indebtedness is about to descend on the American shopping landscape.

Failure to help invest in small, diversified local business growth while deferring to high cost super-malls needs re-thinking. Copy-cat chains that vacuum local money, mostly to be sent to distant headquarters, have become a dominant pattern, not healthy for long range and local urban dynamics. It is a question of proportion and balance.

In the 1950's, there occurred a prophetic exchange of views between the elder Henry Ford and Walter Reuther, the head of the United Auto Workers. "I'd like to see you get some union dues out of these guys," joked Ford, pointing at the very first robotic engine-drilling machines. "That's fine, Henry," replied Reuther. "I'd like to see you sell one a car."

Blaming labor for the culpability of top management, who, for example, continue to market outdated gas-hog automobiles, while exporting know-how and productive jobs overseas, is hardly a mark of national intelligence. Producing money managers at top-ranked colleges, who learn to churn money with nary a thought to creative production, is an economic fantasy. Producing multi-millionaires, even billionaires, while leaving behind a shrinking middle class and an outlandish system of rewards for failure is a formula for continuing decrepitude and social breakdown. It reflects in the obsessive behavior found in the malls, which have become a pseudo-religious experience.

We have to change our ways of doing business and our patterns of consumption and planning if we are to keep abreast of competition with countries that make investment in their people's health, social security, and creative employment a top priority. It is the intelligent way to national security and the pursuit of happiness.

SENIOR ROAD RACING CAN BE A CYCLING EGO TRIP

Both ends of the "seniors" spectrum, from couch potato to over-exerciser, present an extremely bizarre picture. Why should people over forty, even barely 30 years of age, throw in the towel and devote the rest of their once active lives to expanding their waistlines? And perhaps even more puzzling are the senior citizens who go the exact opposite route and make of exercise a power play?

As statistic show, we are fast becoming a nation that finds more pleasure in over-eating and bragging about food consumption than in walking and feeling the joy of movement, the wind in our faces. For a long time these ruinous patterns perplexed me, until one day I realized that the entire consumption model of our society is intimately connected with competitive sports, especially as portrayed on television.

Hold it, you say. Is not the whole sports scene the essence of vigor and activity, the very opposite of sloth? For some people, I am sure this is so. But for the 50,000 and more people in the grandstands watching 18 or 22 people work-out, it is only ceremonially true, as ever more it has become a habit to take "exercise" in an easy chair while swilling beer and chips. What the big games have subtly taught people is that, past mid-twenties, we don't have what it takes to be worth much on the playing field. Indeed, they teach us to forget about our own body health, while slavishly counting points for somebody else's purchased team! It's far easier and more exciting to scream and shout and raise blood pressure over plays, errors, or bold leaps made by a quasi-public or commercial team than take good care of our body (all the way swallowing a barrage of food and drink messages that in most cases are plain unhealthy).

Countless hours in school or afterwards are spent learning how to play by the rules of this or that popular sport, but very few young people learn how to take care of themselves in preparation for 80 percent of their adult life.

You may not like to hear this, but it is true, and the sports pros not only know it but feed upon it. Think what would happen to attendance at the big games if most people decided what to do on a Saturday, Sunday or other big game time based upon what is best for their own health rather than what makes for gate receipts and glory!

At the opposite end of the spectrum are the adult over-exercisers. They may be spectators too, but their retirement life especially is given over to Health, with a capital H- as in Hormones. I've watched with some amusement and not a little concern as my wife and her biking friends pretend to emulate Lance Armstrong. So many, 50 or older, have literally hit the dirt in the past few months that I gave up counting. The local hospitals and clinics are making big business out of their heroic efforts at hurtling over the handlebars, skidding fast on steep downhill curves, being blind-sided by hostile drivers who hate bicyclists, and dropping into ditches while too busily talking. Most wouldn't be seen with a bike that weighs more than 20 pounds, although why taking two pounds off a bicycle is more important than losing ten unneeded body pounds is beyond me.

I remember when biking was recreation, not combat. My longest ride, post high school, was from the Boston suburbs to Lake Sharon in the Blue Hills, some 35 exhausting miles. My bicycle then weighed about 30 pounds and had but a single gear. Nonetheless, it was lots of fun, with much to see, and there was no need to engage my companion in a competitive race. The joy was in going, not in proving anything.

What I have learned over the course of a lifetime of exercise is to be your own person and listen carefully to your own body - not anyone else's. I always think back to a great lesson learned with pain and eventual triumph. As a scrawny sophomore at Illinois, I had spent the winter "beefing up" at the gymnastics-weight-lifting gym next door to the ball-fields. When spring arrived, my teammates spotted me through the window and urged me to come down and practice for the coming season. That was when my health mentor, then an engineering student and a model of physical conditioning, observed that I was being confronted with an ultimate test: "Sometimes" he smiled, "you have to choose between ego and health!"

So why do seniors persist in heavy stress-cycling even at the cost of physical breakdown? For some it is blind self-gratification. For others it is their way of proving they are alive and kicking and have much yet to give to society, the young, their neighbors and friends. As the occupants of a Venice, Calif., senior house told the social worker who asked why they argue so much- "It's to prove we are still keen, still among the living- even if the young so stupidly don't listen to us."

They follow the admonition of the poet, Dylan Thomas: "Rage, rage against the dying of the light." And so it is with the cyclists, who need more to reflect on another poet's sage advice, that of John Ruskin: "There was always more in the world than a man could see, walked he ever so slowly. He will see no more by going fast, for his glory is not in going but in being."

We do need to stretch ourselves, but just as important to plant some roses and be one with the wildflowers and the gentle wind. There's so much to see besides pavement! Cycling as exercise, done as a rhythm with our beautiful world, is a form of spiritual and physical re-awakening. But a bicycle as fetish, and senior road racing just another form of competitive game, amounts to nothing more or less than an ego trip- a great delusion that shadows the greater truth: "the paths of glory lead but to the grave."

JOY OF GETTING BACK TO NATURE
IS NOT A LICENSE TO PLAY SAVAGE

"Who loves the mountains leaves the flowers." Every Swiss mountain train used to carry this caution. Perhaps they still do. The slogan stuck with me over 30 years because of its simple truth: Take wildness where it is and leave it be!

Spring! People are once again flocking to the wild lands. From every city and town, in motor homes, campers, automobiles and motorcycles come hordes of urbanites seeking, supposedly, peace and tranquility.

Yes, it is the call of the wild. Or it was until the wildness in us became civilized. Now throbs a contrary beat, a thirst for all the claptrap of city living, plus the chatter and nervous background that we have grown to feed upon. The fear of quiet and the realization of our own puniness before nature is hard to face. Rather than leave the wild lands be, we insist of "civilizing" them.

Urbanites press to bring ever more roads and city comforts to the great parks and forests. Few simple camps are left, and some national parks look like mall parking lots. A pattern of preening and loud display develops: Motorcycles roar into campgrounds; tourist stores with milling crowds abound; tires crunch on gravel as motor homes maneuver; card games and TV drown out the night sounds and the mystery of the stars. And the human voice babbles on, erasing the hoot of owl, the soothing melody of the distant brook. Quiet is then an aberration, and nature is even viewed as "un-natural."

Thus despoiled is the sanctuary we profess to seek- an escape from the frantic life we lead in our cities. Will wilderness become extinct and the wilderness spirit along with it? Not if we can learn to look at visitation to the wild places as a special game with rules we must learn and steadfastly obey as we do with all other kinds of sport.

The basic rule of the "wilderness game" is one of nature's predominance. By simple definition, a human visitor to the earth's wild places is but a bird of passage. The entry requirement is a promise to leave nothing more than footprints- a cushioned and quiet experience. Getting back to nature is not a license to play savage, certainly not with modern equipment.

The wilderness game is surely different from more familiar sports: no point score or time barrier, no start and finish lines, no leagues and cheering fans, and no TV payoff. But like other sports, the game of wilderness shares a common need for rules of order to prevent disruption and commotion on the playing field.

While not formalized in a rule-book, this play in nature lives off common sense boundaries we can easily recognize. These essential ground rules are trampled upon when forest and parkland become an arena for whirlwind tours and carnival theatre. Actions that smother the quiet call-of-the-wild lands are destructive to plant and animal communities and intrude upon the privacy rights of human visitors.

Consider the effect of disrespect for rules on popular games: Spectators would wander at will onto the field of play. A player could claim a "right" to bat with an oar, another to hit a tennis ball under the net. Loud radios could be used to hassle players at matches. Beer cans would litter the fairways and laundry would hang from clubhouse windows. And greens-flags might be convenient for target practice.

Such intolerable and ludicrous situations would soon end with the appearance of rules-enforcers- umpires, police, the players themselves. To continue play, we would have to agree that the rules are inviolable.

Note, none of this obedience to sport rules is "natural." It is carefully taught in school and on the field, and is the hidden price of entry to the game. We are justifiably annoyed at people who do not care about or don't try to understand the rules. We insist they learn.

The wilderness game is really no different. The need for quiet, the rule of allowing nature to predominate over human activity must be taught in every school and park. It won't be easy!

Recreational sports today are increasingly aggressive and aggression-producing, leading to a swaggering spectatorism. After the mid-twenties, most people dissociate themselves from active participation in games they have been relentlessly taught, and fall back into the passive status of "spectator sports fan." No wonder that yelling and preening, all attention-seeking behaviors, are carried over into other fields of play, into nature's enclaves, where just the opposite goals and rules are called for. It is not surprising that obesity and heart disease abound in a population that has all but abandoned any commitment to lifelong exercise and active involvement with the wild lands.

Our wild places are a national resource, a sustaining and spiritual element in an increasingly pressured world. If they become a ground for playing-out city tensions, urban people will have broken a principal safety valve for mental health. Technologically-driven, super-stimulated urbanites, obsessed with "winning," will increasingly lack compassion and caring about legacy to future generations.

They will be less and less able to differentiate between the wild lands and Disneylands, and will become ever more content with climbing fake mountains and screaming their way through artificial waterfalls. They will scar the rocks and stare at the scenery for a few moments and see little but background and dollar value. And they will pick the wildflowers and bring them home wilted and dying like their own souls.

A caring approach to wilderness, an effort to learn the beauty of quiet, the tranquility of being unplugged from broadcast or canned chatter and noise, can work wonders for our lands and for ourselves. But can we rise to this kind of educational challenge? And do we have the compassion and courage to thrive on being with ourselves unplugged in a setting where nature predominates?

THE TREES OF HIGUERA STREET DOWNTOWN

CRACKS IN THE ECONOMY- THE U.S. AGAINST ITSELF

April- 2005

What is apparent to foreign observers, much less so to Americans, is an underlying instability in the American economy. This threat is a function of gross national over-spending, which shows in private credit card debt, plus a warped and loophole-filled tax system and lack of domestic savings. For too many years there was little inclination in Washington to face the potential economic danger to the country. And as we sink into deeper and deeper debt to Japan, China and other trading nations, the Iraq and Afghanistan gambits with their enormous costs looms as a big part of this economic mess.

On a recent trip to Mexico, a revealing article appeared in a local English language newspaper, subtitled, "Now Economists Say: Watch China." While finding that most Mexicans believe her economy depends on the U.S., edgy observers are finding that export sales to the United States and remittances to Mexican families from Mexican workers in the U.S. (over 16 BILLION dollars in 2004) rests on ... "what is globally seen as perilously soaring U.S. deficits (in 2004 more than $700 billion). Analysts are concerned that foreigners could lose their affinity for dollars. In any rush to dump the dollar, stock prices would collapse causing interest rates to soar- thus dragging down the U.S. economy.

Key Mexican economists have raised cautions and have advised the central bank to convert at least part of their dollar holdings into Euro reserves. But the Mexican government and banks are afraid of worsening relations with the U.S., already strained by Mexican opposition to the war in Iraq and by corruption and crime south of our border.

The feeling in many world financial capitals, is that the growing U.S. deficit, and the failure of the Bush administration to deal with the many dangerous imbalances jeopardizes the entire global economy. The most trenchant critics suggest that the administration is "economically illiterate": "not only can't it read the writing on the wall, but it has not read Chinese writings equating modern economic strategy with true strength. In other words, the Chinese seem to have learned that a healthy economy sustains defense, not necessarily the other way around.

The concern is that as the U.S. exhausts itself in foreign adventures, China is free to gather increasing wealth as well as technological and military robustness. It is said that once prosperous economies (the U.S.) can be pushed into recession and financial turbulence and then "toppled backwards" perhaps ten or more years. China now finances one-third or more of the U.S. deficit, and some Mexican economists worry that should China utilize currency devaluations as an economic thrust and begin cashing in on U.S. treasury debt, both the American and Mexican economies could shatter. Of course China and the U.S. are also co-dependent, and both countries need to nurture a positive partnership.

It did not go unnoticed, the Mexican newspaper notes, that Mexico and China recently signed economic agreements toward "a partnership in cooperation, instead of competitive rivalry," and the two countries are attempting to carry their strategic relationship to a new level. This is smart economics and a good precedent for international relations.

The fear of the U.S. economic blundering is not at all foreign to American soil. In 1960, in a famous warning address to Congress and the American people, President Eisenhower candidly and bluntly reminded us: "Every addition to defense expenditures does not automatically increase military security. Because security is based on moral and economic, as well as purely military strength, a point can be reached at which additional funds for arms, far from bolstering security, weaken it."

With an awakening China at relative peace, her rate of growth far exceeds our own, even as the U.S. weakens itself by displacing jobs and know-how overseas. Our strength and treasury are sapped in foreign adventures of dubious advantage to American society and ideals. In a strange twist of Teddy Roosevelt's admonition, the Bush administration seemed galvanized on "speaking harshly and beating ourselves over the head with a big stick."

American worker's needs are ignored in the lust for low wage overseas labor, while Asian and other poorer workers are viewed as both viable producers and consumers. The China market has become a Washington obsession. All but forgotten is the fact that the economic sword cuts both ways; lost jobs at home in production and middle-management leave a large group of formerly well-to-do consumers holding an empty bag. It's a strange case of self-defeatism. As the old song goes, "When will they ever learn?" *-Unpublished*

CALHOUN IS ALIVE!
NEUTRALIZING THE FEDERAL GOVERNMENT

The George W. Bush program cut to the heart of federal-state responsibilities and went beyond the New Federalism of Ronald Reagan or the policies of the elder George H.W. Bush. All three feel more a throwback to that old states' rights proponent of the mid 19th century, John C. Calhoun.

Reagan's New Federalism yielded a dramatic decrease in the role of federal supervision of the marketplace (deregulation), severe cuts in public sector spending except for national defense, major reductions in federal corporate taxes in the shaky effort to fuel private sector investment, and, most important for consideration of federal-state balance, a transfer from the federal government to the states of long-established responsibility for and financing of many public programs.

Looking back to the period between the Great Depression and Reaganomics, there had emerged a virtual iron law of government and politics: the absence of effective state and local action to deal with problems of national importance in public health, education, safety, and welfare invites federal attention. Sooner or later, federal money and power would flow into the vacuum, with examples as far ranging as programs for nutrition, urban housing, transportation, coastal planning, rodent control, alcoholism, education, and medical research. Often, nearly bankrupt American cities, as well as some states, became more and more dependent on federal stimulus money.

As even conservative President Eisenhower explained after five years of struggle attempting to limit federal program expansion, "In each instance state inaction or inadequate action…has forced emergency federal action." Candidly he remarked that the states view federal programs mainly from their own particular economic interest and not from the viewpoint of national concern.

The elder President Bush tried to do what Eisenhower was unable to do, but was diverted and ultimately undone by the first war with Iraq and the $300 billion dollar federal deficit it helped produce. President Clinton was able to re-introduce an activist federal role and at the same time greatly reduce the national debt and leave behind him a huge budget surplus. Rather than being an incentive to the younger

President Bush and his cohorts, the budget surplus came as a frightening challenge: How could they de-fund the federal government so that it could not engage in program action that ran against the minimalist philosophy of government that Bush partisans embraced? It took less than one year for them to reduce the federal budget surplus to zero.

The events of September 11, 2001 gave the Bush team a shock, but also a bonus. The shock we have all shared. But the bonus came in the way of a handy excuse to still further reduce the role of federal government in domestic concerns other than issues of security. By 2002, the focus has been shifted mainly to Iraq and oil supplies and to homeland security in a declared endless war against terrorism. Billions of dollars that might be spent on domestic problems were routinely pushed aside under the guise of war priority. Deficit spending, sometimes the enemy of Republican budget-balancers, soon was seen as having a silver lining. And much of the public, even now, has been blind-sided by the smokescreen.

Despite the need then for strengthened national security, the Bush-team strategy was fundamentally at war with itself. The solar energy research budget, perhaps the one key path to energy independence from mid-east oil, has been reduced by more than half. Gas-guzzling cars became all the rage and the federal government was totally passive on the issue. Despite massive evidence of global warming by scientists from a hundred nations, the Bush administration continued to back the oil and coal industry line that there is not enough evidence of human causation. And so it went. Program after program of generally routine federal development and action was sidelined, reduced, or struck down in the interest of tightening the noose on federal research and social program spending that didn't conform to the pre-set political agenda of the administration in Washington.

For president G.W. Bush, as for Reagan and the elder president Bush, the primary concern domestically was retrenching federal power. A century and a half earlier, John C. Calhoun, the fiery South Carolinian advocate of states' rights, (pre-Civil War) claimed that a proper federalism meant preventing the accretion of the powers of national government from the outset. In his time, Calhoun argued correctly for the principle of equality of treatment of states and sections by the government in Washington. His arguments, however, went awry as he came to defend states' rights more in terms of what the federal government cannot or should not do than in terms of the mutual obligations of both state and national government to promote the general welfare of the people.

Senator (and Vice President) Calhoun saw the national good as simply the sum of separate state options and efforts, and thus became ensnared in the legal fiction of U.S. government as a compact between sovereign states. This led to the doctrine of "nullification,"- the supposed right of states to have discretion in deciding what acts of Congress to obey or not obey, and thus denying the ultimate power of the Federal judiciary clearly defined in Article III of the Constitution. It took a civil war to institutionalize implementation of federal authority.

The Bush team was perennially disturbed by federal activism in promotion of a social, as contrasted to a military agenda. But even here they were hypocritical in pushing federal power into selected areas of personal concern (abortion and family planning; support for religious education; right of privacy etc.) Far more than in Calhoun's time, the federal government remains unfair in distributing spending among the states. Fewer than ten states have the political bark to gain fair access to the national purse. Both states and the local jurisdictions (cities and towns) have lost some degree of dynamism because of the decline in national investment and financial aid from Washington.

The continued growth in poverty and joblessness, the lack of affordable housing, the rot in our cities, the bottlenecks in transportation, the inadequacy of our service economy and general economic health are directly tied to inadequate federal investment and less than viable national and state policies. Defense appropriations again have become a tail that wags the budget dog and robs social programs of their lifeblood.

History demonstrates that both sectionalism and grave social cleavage result from static federal government in the face of state and local inaction and financial incapacity. The economy of the country degrades and implodes as a function of declining federal (and state) research and development. Instead, public money is expended mainly in areas targeted by powerful political lobbies. Alternative energy and solar power, high speed rail, low cost housing, infrastructure repair and preventative maintenance, school expansion and modernization, enforcement of environmental protection laws, and health care are

163

examples of areas long suffering under the restrictive views of "new federalism".

What was new about the Bush plan for America is not the so-called "new federalism," but is the resurgence of selective antipathy to federal authority and the nihilistic consequences it bears for all of us. How and with what success the Obama administration will move differently remains to be seen.

-Unpublished

IN TIMES OF DISPUTE, TRY MEDIATION

Conflict mediation involves an amazing variety of situations and cases:

The young man wants his engagement ring returned, but his former beau says that she need not return it or its value in hard cash because he was the initiator of the breakup.

The gentleman is filled with anger toward the owner of the huge dog who bit his little Poopsie, and he wants payment for the pain and suffering caused as well as an abject apology. The owner of the larger dog is humble about apologizing but claims that the whole incident was the result of a utility worker leaving the yard gate wide open.

The architect and his client are at odds over "reasonable payment" for design changes, while in another mediation room the landlord and his departing student tenants are hassling over the cost of cleanup and renovation and how much can legitimately be held back from the security deposit.

The parent and adult child can barely speak to each other and seek neutral ground to soothe and direct the verbal traffic. Then there are neighbor disputes over the legitimacy of road grading and repair and apportioning attendant costs, or a case where the planting of expensive bamboo along a property line blocked the view from an adjoining home. And so it goes, in countless variations, both in court or in private mediation rooms. In most cases, a monetary settlement is sought.

The key to successful mediation is unlocking the parties from their self-justification so they can listen to and validate each other. A court or arbitrator would hear both sides and issue a judgment or ruling. Somebody will lose. But mediation is different. It is voluntary and, guided by a trained mediator, the parties must try and reach their own settlement- one that is acceptable to both sides.

This is not easy, but mediated settlements have been found to be more effective at resolving disputes and easing the impasse that generates so much hostility and frustration.

The key rules of engagement in mediation are simple:

- Participants must be open to negotiation

- We may sing together but we talk only one at a time.

- Be respectful and listen to the other side. Take notes, if you wish, and make your rebuttal or comment when your time comes.

- After the mediator has your stories clear, be prepared to engage in healthy, probing discussion.

- Know that all is private in mediation, and the mediators cannot be made legal witnesses nor can they take sides.

- Agreements reached under court mediation will be validated as part of the court record.

Emotional upset is often a part of the process, and it is better for participants to express it by putting feelings about a situation on the table rather than stuffing them and harboring resentments. Here is where we, mediators and participants, enter what I call the "red zone," a time usually toward the early part of the mediation when tempers may still be raw. The potential for explosive reactions to things said by the other side are always lurking and need to be carefully watched through facial and postural cues.

Otherwise, one or another participant may suddenly decide to end the discussion with a closing outburst or by angrily stomping off. This occurred in the dog-bite case, previously noted, and just after the owner of the large dog (the biter) had expressed his remorse over what had happened. I had noticed some scowling on the part of Poopsie's owner while the apology was given, yet was surprised when the gentleman suddenly snarled, "Too little and too late!" as he rushed out of the room.

Mediators must remind participants that they are going to hear things from the other side that they might find hard to digest. But in fact, that is partly why they are present- to listen and to fairly entertain a different point of view. "Make notes on things with which you agree or disagree and prepare to explain your position considerately."

Once a considerate state of discussion is implanted, movement toward the green zone of democratic dialogue is probably assured. Mediation, after all, is a rising toward the highest human potential for conciliatory action and problem solving. In times of conflict we all need to drop our defensiveness, settle down, and give mediation a fair try.

SINGLE ISSUE AND BLOCK VOTING
IN PRESIDENTIAL ELECTIONS

Three to ten percent of adult Americans classify themselves as vegetarians, according to sampling studies by food marketers. To date there is no block or en masse voting by vegetarians for a candidate for the presidency of the U.S. However, given the current political winds, it is possible that at some time in the near future it might become strategic for vegetarians to use their focus on gastronomical preferences and animal rights to support the one candidate for president who agrees with them.

Today there is a fusion of activists over abortion, religion, gender, guns etc. -- special interest partisans who are willing, separately or together, to ignore or throw to the wind all transcendent national-Constitutional issues; transfixed by a particular passion, they define their nomination or general election vote almost solely in terms of a litmus test on the one main issue dear to their heart. That voters of a particular persuasion have a right to do so is obvious. But in terms of the national interest and of an intelligent weighing of what is the greater good for the country, it is, unfortunately, tunnel vision. It distorts and eventually smothers the free market arena of democratic politics by creating "tipping points" which freeze out attempts at rational discourse.

If each interest groups adopt this block voting strategy, the country would deadlock and begin to come apart at the seams- much as what happened in the great pre-Civil War struggles over slavery and the tariff -- issues which were allowed to grow and fester in a way that distorted discourse and threw sand in the machinery of mediated politics and government.

No significant portion of the American electorate can block-vote without somehow crimping the hose that feeds democratic politics. Hot potato examples abound including single-issue partisans of gun control, abortion, sexual identity, gay marriage, abolition of the income tax, gambling and many basically state issues. Race too enters the picture from a different angle; black people, for example, who have good historical reasons for distrusting our political system, may vote for a candidate solely because of a like skin color. But it has the same disruptive effect on political balance as when larger groups of white people reject a black candidate on the basis of race.

There ARE valid over-riding national issues- a sinking economy, health care, war -facing the American Republic today! To snuff these out of the political choice arena because of the obsession with one or two passions, however legitimate, is lunacy. Often masked in the name of moral identity, obsessive single-issue voting is both sanctimonious and destructive. It makes a farce of the political process under the guise of "morality"- and can be the kind of patriotic purity that might be defined as the last refuge of a scoundrel. It takes the voter's eye off national fundamental concerns and fogs the opportunity for sound rational policy-making.

There is no quick or easy answer as to how to thwart the growing tendency toward band-wagon voting and single issue politics. The hammering of very costly advertising with its attendant hysteria trivializes and dumbs-down real debate. Computer generated propaganda messages add to the mess of peripheral issues and sleazy ploys.

A six-month campaign limit and strictly controlled spending would be excellent steps toward a sane electoral process with targeted focus on over-arching national issues. Sooner than we think there are relatively few days left until the start of the next 2-year presidential campaign. That's enough to make anyone gag.

The educational system also bears much of the blame for the political blockage that exists today. Regurgitation-learning destroys focus on critical thinking and sharpened judgment. By teaching mainly to the test, the schools and universities insure the citizenry flunks en masse when it comes to civic responsibility, historical knowledge and political awareness. Block voting feeds on this. Like the greenhouse effect, we ignore the coming tides at our peril. *—Unpublished*

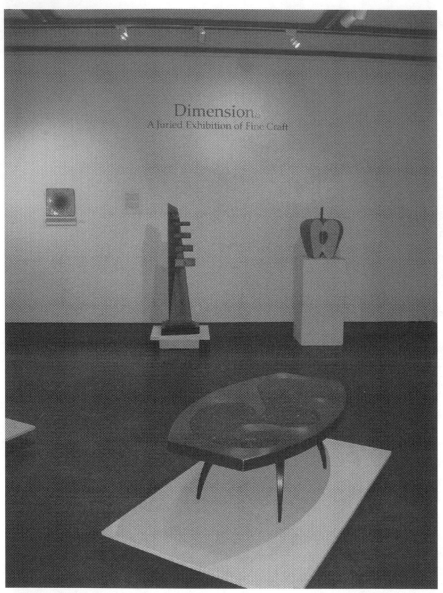

ANOTHER LOOK AT THE CRAFT EXHIBIT, SLO ART CENTER

HANDS OFF HANDSHAKES

When the cold and flu season is hard upon us, we must think defensively about all our non-hygienic habits, even those we do almost subconsciously.

After incontrovertible evidence proved that smoking is a health menace, it took more than twenty years before the risk was acknowledged in law. Still, teenagers and even adults who should know better, continue to light up, but with the onus now fully upon them. Today, non-smokers have laws granting them the right to complain and restrict smoking areas, and also block the effects of second-hand smoke.

But what about another unhealthy habit, encouraged as a common mark of politeness itself. Yes, I speak of greeting by shaking hands, an old custom from frontier days when an empty right hand indicated the lack of a weapon and a peaceful intent. Is that hand really so empty, just because it has no obvious armament? The scientific fact is that hand is likely loaded with cold and flu bacteria and viruses, especially during the colder months. Study after study has confirmed that even more than airborne sneeze droplets, the most likely source of transmission of colds and flu are human hands and all that they contact.

Hidden camera studies reveal that in a five- or 10-minute period, we tend to put our hands to our nose many times. This subconscious habit is such a normal part of life, we don't take notice of its negative consequences. In the cold and flu season, it is a sure way of passing on infection under the guise of cheer and goodwill. And with the newer strains of flu, we must learn to be doubly careful about hygiene.

"Wash your hands often with hot soapy water," we are told by health authorities. But even that warning message has becomes a generality that has little follow-through. What they should be telling us is to stop the antiquated habit of hand-shaking as a greeting, and to substitute some gesture more harmless such as a wave of a raised hand. It will take a while to get a new gesture established and accepted. Meanwhile, I suggest simply saying to the person with the outstretched hand, "No offense intended, but I don't shake hands in the cold and flu season."

What about the person with the fancy linen handkerchief? It's more likely to be a male, who whips it out and waves or snaps it in the air (to get the dust out?) before applying it to his nose for a loud "blow." Likely, he's been carefully pocketing his collection of bacteria-ridden snot for days or more, and has little thought for the consequences of his act for those around him. Can we politely suggest a disposable tissue packet? After all, we have to choose health over habit.

A recent incident: Six friends showed up for a dinner invitation. One person arrived sneezing and red-eyed. She laughed it off as she hugged and shook hands with everyone: "Don't worry, nothing serious; I just have a little cold." Three days later, three of the five guests were cold-ridden. Their nasal discharges and hand movements passed the infection on to their children and to wives and husbands. And doubtless then was relayed on the job, in schools, among friends. All because one selfish individual would not stay at home and avoid contact. Her gift for the season was to pass on a week of sneezing and exhaustion to an ever-widening circle. Of course, everyone was too embarrassed to say anything to her when she arrived. And she had not the sense to warn them beforehand and to stay away.

We have to become more aware of our avoidable, unhealthy habits. The dollar loss alone of such infections are staggering. The misery quotient runs very high. And it's not just hand-shaking, but hygiene in general that has gone awry. In Japan, people routinely wear cold-masks when sick. I've observed that only a quarter of the men in my "health club" even bother to wash their hands after using the toilet. Then they use all the equipment. Add to that the snorters and boisterous sinus clearers one confronts everywhere.

I end with a cautionary limerick:

There once was a man from Wheeling,
Who had manners not appealing;
A sign on the door said,
"Don't spit on the floor."
So he carefully spat on the ceiling.

IS AUTO INSURANCE REALLY 'INSURANCE'?

After more than 45 years of no moving accidents and no insurance claims, fate caught up with me.

My wife had driven away from home to complete some errands. But unbeknownst to me as I entered the garage with our dog in tow, she had forgotten something and hurriedly returned home. She parked temporarily just outside the garage, in a spot which we had agreed never to park, and entered the house through the front door. I looked in my mirror and in my mind saw nothing unusual. I pressed the garage-opener and backed three feet, hitting her car at about 3 mph, and doing about $2,300 in damages.. Neither car was even close to the street. Her car was unoccupied and no one was injured. Both cars were fully insured and by the same company.

My insurance company was quick to respond, directing us to a body shop, and the matter was soon settled and our cars beautifully fixed over the next few weeks. But the matter of insurance did not end there.

As I understand insurance, it works on the theory of spreading the risk. Many people become policy-holders, of which only a relative few have accidents and make claims. Supposedly, the policy-holders without claims are the pot that pays insurance to the claimants. The difference between what the insurance company takes in (the premiums) and what they pay out in claims is legitimate company profit for the risk they take.

But I soon learned that it doesn't really work that way. Despite my long years of lack of claims, I was declared in effect a "higher risk driver" and my insurance was increased approximately $750 for the next three years. Seven hundred fifty times three equals approximately the money the insurance company paid out to fix the body damage on our cars.

I phoned my insurance company and asked how this system could possibly be called "insurance"? - especially as I have been paying insurance premiums for so many years without a claim. They explained that their action is justified on the basis of my higher risk as a driver. Does this mean, I asked, that if I drive accident free for the next three years that you will refund the "risk money" to me? Hardly.

Well, I commented, you are not really in the insurance business, but appear more to be in the loan business. You loan me the money to fix my car and gradually take it back in installments. Indeed, if I knew this and decided to pay the entire cost of the accident by myself, you would not know anything about the accident and I would not be branded a "risky driver."

That is so, commented the polite insurance representative. If you care to look it at that way, that is fine, but be assured that all insurance companies increase the rates of those who have accidents. And so I leave you with the question: Is automobile insurance really "insurance"? And is the consumer being stiff-armed?

ENTRANCE TO THE DOWNTOWN CENTRE,
WITH STATUE OF PUCK

THE HIGH COST OF UNCRITICAL TEACHING

The costs of education make up a large part of every city and state budget. In California, education has a priority draw on funding. But what are we buying with all the hundreds of millions of dollars expended on primary and secondary schools and in state support for varied levels of colleges and universities? What do we expect our students to learn, and how seriously do we expect our teachers to create the qualities of mind that make education a vital investment? The last question is rarely asked in deliberations over finance. Yet, it must be addressed if we are to avoid a huge waste of taxpayer dollars and lost investments in educational inputs and outputs, as well as in precious time itself.

Educational sterility stems from a general failure to teach most people how to learn. I am not speaking about copying and note-taking or performing well on multiple-choice tests, but of engaging in dialogue and critical thinking.

Educators often ask: Why can't my students think for themselves? Why are they so unprepared and so often intellectually lazy? Why do they expect me to do their thinking for them? If the truth be known, relatively few teachers and professors are using the kinds of materials and the discussion strategies that would build in their students a mental set and a taste for critical thinking. Typical classroom atmosphere and procedures —mainly taking notes, copying, looking up answers in a textbook and recalling information dull the possibilities for creating the very qualities of mind that educators avow as their goal. There is little emphasis on the evaluation of knowledge or the promotion of intellectual curiosity, with most of the time available for discussion dominated by teacher and professor talk. Left as passive, often bored spectators, with little opportunity to evaluate the information presented or to make critical judgments, students turn off intellectually and simply go through the motions necessary to complete the course; many are content to play this education game as it requires little intellectual effort on their part.

Teachers and students commonly miss the point that the opposite of critical thinking is "uncritical thinking", which is really not thinking at all! A diet of uncritical "thinking" eventually fosters the kinds of technological and policy blunders that we see featured in the daily news.

Why spend years in school to learn to run with the herd and spout the commonplace? Such banter is really better characterized as "bull" and is, perhaps, an easy way to pass the time. In thinking critically, by contrast, we seek to penetrate to the core of an issue or problem. Thinking critically includes the following:

- An ability to raise important questions and explore alternatives;

- A keen sense of what is missing or needed to solve a problem;

- An ability to deal with complexity and to form hypotheses;

- A sensitivity to the background of an issue;

- A knack for separating important information from material that is peripheral or less relevant;

- A healthy skepticism and a corresponding ability and willingness to test one's theories and explore one's feelings;

- A willingness to challenge and be challenged; an ear for what others are saying and an ability to step into another person's shoes.

Basically there are two types of teachers – senders and receivers. Senders dominate the teaching ranks, and are primarily concerned with what they are going to tell the class about the subject under study. Receivers are more concerned with the questions they are going to pose and how to make the learners an active part of the process. Senders focus on their own ability to explain information and give answers; receivers focus on how the class will process the problem presented and what the learners will contribute to the dialogue by way of insightful judgments and solutions. Senders tend to concentrate on organizing their notes and lectures, while receivers relate more to organizing an inquiry process and preparing for active listening. In brief, senders tell and receivers ask.

Many educators erroneously view the difference between these two polar teacher types as a matter of the importance placed on knowledge, as though only the senders are concerned with rigorous academic preparation and subject content. In truth, both types of teachers, senders and receivers, are inextricably involved with both subject content and method, although in very different ways. Indeed, there is sender and receiver in all of us! However, it is also true that the traditional image and role of the teacher or professor is misidentified with sending. Say the word "teacher" and the image projected is of a man or woman at the head of a class pointing, telling, explaining, while the students listen, absorb, regurgitate. When the traditional sender-teacher signals the class he is ready to receive, he commonly expects either a question on which he can begin sending answers once again, or a carbon copy explanation along the lines of what he has already told the class.

Let us step back and consider the Chinese proverb: "I listen and I forget; I see and I remember; I do and I understand." What so many educators tend to forget is that learners only imperfectly remember material set forth in lecture and like witnesses to an event, they perceive different aspects of the subject or scene. Listening and watching are important, but learning involves much more than that. The human capacity to absorb and remember is imperfect at best, even haphazard, and is subject to all kinds of perceptual selection and distortion. Senders seem surprised by these perceptual deficiencies so obvious in students and they often complain about "the inability of today's learners." They forget the long rehearsal hours that went into their own preparation and gloss over their own forgetting rate. They review their notes. They fail to recognize that the teacher is almost the only one in the room who is intellectually active and reinforcing his learning by acting as chief learner. Thus the adage, "If you want to learn something difficult to remember, teach it!"

The true measure of effective teaching is not simply what the teacher does, how he or she stands and delivers. The full measure of teaching includes what the learners receive in the way of both improved critical capacity and knowledge. Teaching implies this full measure of learning, or it makes little sense. It's akin to watching a baseball game with an active pitcher but no batter, or listening to a symphony in which there is an active conductor, but no orchestra. Much time spent in what is loosely called "education" is simply wasted and a lost and perhaps foolish investment.

Sending and receiving is a balancing process for both learner and learned, and not a closed circuit beginning and ending at the teacher's desk. The well-balanced, artful teacher knows the value of open questioning and aims at a discovery process which activates the learners. To be a fine teacher, one must be in love with good questions. Teaching is much more than giving and receiving right answers. Memorizing "right answers" is hardly a high order of thinking, to say nothing of the forgetting rate of learners. As educator Robert Hutchins reflected, "Conclusions cannot really be understood apart from the arguments by which they were reached."

Of course, there are times for the teacher to speak from authority (expertise gained from years of study), to clarify the question and provide short explanations. But given the propensity of teachers to fall back on sending, there are many more times for teacher silence —strategic wait-times used to prompt the inquiry process, allowing thought to jell. The analysis of problems and case studies, the opening of an active process of critical thinking, acts as a catalyst and glue that helps the retention of facts. Then facts become useful tools rather than isolated products spewed forth and soon forgotten. Problem-centered teaching is thus the key to balance between sending and receiving.

Successful teaching requires skill in the art of questioning and listening. When surface skimming of content takes the place of inquiry, there is no real penetration of the arguments set for discussion. Readings are too often a summary of conclusions and, more often than not, fail to pose problems. A majority of textbooks fall into this category. Without the needed critical context, discussion is trivialized. The class is dragged through the teaching hour instead of being activated in a search for answers.

Good timing is the key to heightening the learning process. The teacher must constantly be awake to cues, visual and oral, from the learners and must show considerable patience in asking questions and waiting for responses. Silence is often golden as learners learn to cogitate. The test for the teacher is: How can I best stimulate and sharpen the dialogue? The test for the student is equally challenging: How can I hone my thinking about the problem at hand, rather than wait for the teacher to give out "right answers".

The answer to the oft-heard complaint about limited critical capacity of students is not more lectures, more drill, and more "going back to the basics". We have heard enough of that song over the last forty years or more to insure stalemate in educational planning and continued narcolepsy in the classroom. Educational reform cannot grow out of day-dreams about the "good old days" which were known for similar complaints. It's a blind alley, analogous to what Santayana once said of the fanatic: "One who redoubles his effort when he has forgotten his aim.

Great teachers enliven classroom dialogue, thereby increasing motivation and sharpening analysis. Discussion will always be the anvil upon which the spark of truth is struck. The pulse of great teaching beats strongly in asking, much more than in telling. The telling, while sometimes critical, is the easy part of teaching that can more easily be taken over by computers and new technology. Inquiry and problem-orientation will always remain as human arts with the greatest scientific and civilizing potential. We have to move on and reform education so that it becomes a truly worthwhile investment.

The fundamental difference between sending and receiving, between preaching and teaching is evident in the light of what we know about how people learn. The preacher has found the truth and is driven to make you believe. In contrast, the teacher seeks the truth and tries to help sharpen your critical mind.

How many of we educators are in the right profession?

Ira Winn: THE EDUCATION MIRAGE (New York: iUniverse, Inc.) expanded comments.

ERODING BLUFFS AND DRIFTING FOG AT
MONTANA DE ORO STATE PARK

THE POLITICS OF DISUNITY

At times, the utter silliness of the health care debate is seen in television and newspaper interviews with Americans who are totally opposed to any federal regulation of the health care marketplace. By and large most people love their Medicare and Social Security programs, but many admit to not knowing that these are federally financed and run. Some are convinced that the government is incapable of running anything, despite a host of contrary examples, ranging from the Peace Corps, Center for Disease Control, Clean Water Act and Headstart for schools, to name but three. Self-contradictory beliefs have been passed around by ignorant pundits who would rather sow disunion under the guise of neutral commentary than try to bring about a true meeting of the minds to solve an urgent national problem.

These selective disenchantments, illogical and politically driven as they may sometimes be, are an unfortunate legacy of three recent administrations, which preached that government is not the solution, but is the problem. No huge public outcry developed, akin to the angry, raucus town hall meetings over health-care, when President Reagan symbolically had the solar panels removed from the White House roof or when subsequent solar energy research and development budgets were cut in half. The public was largely dumbed out. In the name of the supposed greater efficiency of private enterprise, the nation has been stuck in dependence on mid-east oil to this very day.

Following this kind of bizarre, anti-federal logic, we might well argue that the Coast Guard should be abolished because it tells boat owners what they have to do to comply with safety regulations. Or perhaps do away with intelligence gathering because of the failure of security agencies to successfully track the 9/11 hi-jackers.

Or sell off the national parks. How foolish can we get?

A great lesson can be learned from the dilemma that faced President Lincoln on the eve of outbreak of the Civil War. In his First Inaugural Address, facing a mounting wave of protest against the federal government, and largely from the southern states, he appealed for calmness and reason: "In your hands, my dissatisfied fellow countrymen, and not in mine, is the momentous issue of civil war. The government will not assail you. You can have no conflict without being yourselves the aggressors.

You have no oath registered in heaven to destroy the government, while I shall have the most solemn one to preserve, protect, and defend it'. We are not enemies, but friends. We must not be enemies. Though passion may have strained, it must not break our bond of affection...." Lincoln ended by appealing to "the better angels of our nature."

But the hotheads prevailed, as we should know from history. As one caustic observer remarked of the furor raised for independence in South Carolina; "It's too small to be an independent republic, and too large to be a lunatic asylum." The cries of disunity, distortion, and rancorous ignorance led to 600,000 American deaths in a terrible war to save the Union.

Hopefully, we are today a nation that thrives on challenge and deliberation. Unlike many struggling nations, we are not afraid of honest discussion. But discussion can die very quickly when it is allowed to become raucous and mean spirited, when pushed by television and radio mockery and computer rumor. When the exchange of ideas is clouded by hostile voices and hysterical partisanship, facts and arguments have no fair chance to be pondered and appraised. In these times, the huge corporate banking and investment interests, which have taken unparalleled loans from the federal treasury, also stir the airwaves with rhetorical dust and blither, whose aim is to distract the public from a recent history of investment scams and outrageous bonuses and profits borne on the backs of the American public. No positive outcome can result from a system that generates multi-millionaires at the cost of de-financing and ruining the American economic base. Where is the loyalty to the national good in all that?

Almost everyone would like to see a better and fairer health-care system in the U.S. There is room for honest differences of opinion on how best to get there, but we need to do away with mudslinging and rancid innuendo. We have to respect the free marketplace of ideas, or risk falling into the pit of mob psychology, egomania and ultimate sterility. Feeding disunion with ignorance is not a path to strength and greatness as a nation. Not only can we do better than what we have seen recently, but we must BE better.

Unpublished

WHO POSES A GREATER THREAT TO SOCIETY?

Illiteracy is one of our national problems, and not just the inability to read and write, but what is loosely called *cultural illiteracy* or the lack of common understandings. Illiterates lead vastly diminished lives. Nonetheless, and however illiteracy is defined, I conclude that the illiterate are much less a threat to society than the literate.

We have the example of chief executives of multi-national corporations, of great banking and financial empires, who not only falsified their company books, but purposely deceived their own workers and their families, their stockholders, and subverted the very foundations of employment in countries near and far. Because of the sheer size and worldwide reach of their enterprises, inevitably they gravely affect the national economy and erode or destroy public trust in both business and government.

What kind of training was given and absorbed by these chief executives? Where did they get their formal education? And why is the relation of education to implanting ethical values not particularly seen in our society as great a question for investigation as illiteracy, non-voting, or alleged crimes or aberrant behavior by celebrities?

It is the highly educated, often the best and the brightest, who pose a far greater danger to society and democratic institutions precisely because they sit in or near the seats of power, and, as history reveals, make decisions inimical to democratic values and to the future of the planet. Whether it is the corruption or vested interest politics, the blindness of technological arrogance, or the warping pressures of money and power and its effects on the human ego, the educated have demonstrated they are likely to succumb.

The latest scandals of Wall Street and the trillions of dollar indebtedness of our treasury are deadly symbols of a society amiss. The current economic meltdowns of financial and related manufacturing empires poison the marketplace; add the Iraq-Afghanistan gambits to a sad list of fuzzy contracting awards, prison warehousing, the on-going health care crisis, the continuing failure to face up to the realities of global warming, and the unsustainable and economically destructive race to plunder the earth of resources that together add up to a failure of the educational system to train for critical thinking. The liberal arts have been downplayed at our peril. Graduate business and law schools particularly, bear the onus for ineffective training and for patterns of self-serving management that lacks an ethical base and a planetary vision.

It is failure marked by the seeming inability of the graduates, in far too many tests of character, to yield to relevant and primary public interest, to measure long run consequences, and increasingly to pander to money and not to be willing to speak truth to power.

Cronyism and payoff at top levels of government and business management and a hostility to dissenting opinion are signal indictments. The failure to deal preventively and effectively with climate destabilization and other environmental danger signs is perhaps the best current measure of the ineffectiveness of higher education. Indeed, the system seems warped toward generating technological fixes and fixers, rather than producing a generation grounded in humanistic values and a broad and long view toward problem-prevention

The popular delusion that education is a passport to riches more than an awakening to service to society and stewardship of the planet is disturbing and dangerous to our future prosperity and happiness. As things now operate, secondary and higher education are segmented and flat. The universities blame the secondary schools for poor preparation; the secondary schools blame the elementary, which, in turn, blame the parents; the latter return the compliment by blaming both teachers and the schools and colleges. Always abundant are problems of the economy and society which are invoked as valid disclaimers of guilt for all concerned, and everyone thus escapes responsibility for taking the lead in reforming education. That requires working together, demanding intelligent leadership, and getting rid of phony concepts of status and place. Certainly, it would also require a hard look at TV.

Television, perhaps more even than movies, has become the biggest challenge to books and schooling. Although TV can lay claim to some important educational virtues, by and large it has become a distraction from serious thought. Its bill of fare is heavily weighted toward the unseemly, the peripheral, the violent. It is the super-popular medium for the quick fix-- barren stories, empty characters. Tens of millions of young and old are conditioned to watch an endless parade of bad taste and worse art as a daily routine. By constant drumming the abusive and the sordid into home life, it has made violence as American as cherry pie. It justifies the predilections it produces on the basis of public demand-truly a chicken-egg dilemma: which came first?

The profit drive of the broadcast industry recognizes few constraints, as each escalation of the unseemly, in the race for ratings and dollars, begs for a further erosion of standards of good fare. TV violence especially is an electronic drug that cannot be the neutral influence claimed by its purveyors, who are, it must be noted, largely university trained. Although there are great programs on television, they are the exception and their audience is usually not huge.

Colleges and schools have failed to take TV seriously, at least to the point of teaching how to be alert and intelligent consumers of media. And the cult of youth in high schools and colleges feasts on media image and hype and marginal surrogates who model a lost and silly condition. It is a special world of titillation, of conformity to passing fads and sounds, and to ultimately boring meanderings. It helps segregate the young from adults and adulthood, encouraging a teen groupie sub-culture almost antagonistic to a transition to adult life. Thus television helps create and fuel the irregular pulse of society, feeds it with aberrant image, and throws in an occasional real bone.

The educated have proven too often parochial in view, hypnotized by a money ethic, and short of imagination and ethical perspective. Who would have believed that in six years time, two ivy league university graduates would bring the American presidency into two completely different kinds of crisis that reflect their inadequate training in making judgments? Who would have thought that after finally extricating ourselves from the quagmire of Vietnam, that American leadership would still believe in the efficacy of our building, controlling and remaking Iraq or Afghanistan in our own image? Such scenarios are perhaps worthy of comic opera, but hardly that of historically aware men and women with sharpened judgment. Lust for control of oil plus self-delusion about the paths of glory illustrate once again the corruption of power and a lack of sagacity at dealing with illusory thinking.

If we are to reform the educational system into something more than a credentialing organ based on the literacy of game-show players and the snobbery of degrees, we have to vastly improve the product of our schools and universities. Not that they fail to produce well-meaning people, but they fail to filter and prepare those many eventual competitor captains who graduate and go on to command giant enterprises of various kinds, and who give little respect to ethical standards and the concept of stewardship of our planet.

We are moving rapidly in and toward an Old World model of education, complete with a mania for state-mandated testing that dulls or sterilizes good teaching. The educational reform commissions, many led by highly educated and well-meaning people, with lots of big money behind them, fail to recognize the limitations of testing and the enormous burdens of teaching. Together with technocratic over-specialization, the push is toward an eventual feudal stagnation, a two-tier class system in which educational institutions will become less and less centers for criticism or renewal. For too long now, passing multiple-choice exams has becomes the proof of educational competence.

Educational institutions today are far more efficient at and intent upon teaching the pursuit of private gain and competitive struggle for personal ends than in instilling the importance of public obligation and conservation, to say nothing about the art of democratic dialogue and sharpened judgment. The symptoms of these failings and the decline in awareness of their long run reverberations can be seen in the myths of power and performance we seem to live by. The powerful negative resonance of the educated poses a serious danger to the social fabric of the nation and found almost weekly reported in the news. In three hundred years, our country has gone from denial of the divine right of kings to what novelist William Faulkner observed as a self-inflicted despotism of the glands. The outpouring of the educational system may be fine for producing bean counters and status –driven muck-a-mucks, but they won't be capable of doing the kind of thinking and outreach that is required for a civilized society to gain balance and develop in a healthy and inspiring way.

Can we turn the ship of state around? The answer depends on what kind of path and what priorities we are willing and able to embrace.

END